INTRODUCTION TO
OPERA

PAUL TERRY

R•RHINEGOLD
EDUCATION

www.rhinegoldeducation.co.uk

Music Study Guides

GCSE, AS and A2 Music Study Guides (AQA, Edexcel and OCR)
GCSE, AS and A2 Music Listening Tests (AQA, Edexcel and OCR)
GCSE, AS and A2 Music Revision Guides (AQA, Edexcel and OCR)
AS/A2 Music Technology Study Guide (Edexcel)
AS/A2 Music Technology Listening Tests (Edexcel)
AS and A2 Music Technology Revision Guides (Edexcel)

Also available from Rhinegold Education

Musicals in Focus, Baroque Music in Focus, Film Music in Focus
Understanding Popular Music
Careers in Music
Dictionary of Music in Sound

First published 2014 in Great Britain by
Rhinegold Education
14-15 Berners Street
London W1T 3LJ, UK
www.rhinegoldeducation.co.uk

© 2014 Rhinegold Education
a division of Music Sales Limited

Introduction to Opera
Order No. RHG405
ISBN: 978-1-78038-247-0

Exclusive Distributors:
Music Sales Ltd
Distribution Centre, Newmarket Road
Bury St Edmunds, Suffolk IP33 3YB, UK

Printed in the EU

CONTENTS

*In loving memory of Susan Gohren (née Terry), formerly of
the wardrobe department of English National Opera.*

Preface

Opera ranks among the most exciting spectacles that humans can enjoy. Music can convey emotions, create moods and portray the inner feelings and desires of characters in a drama in ways more powerful than words alone.

This book explains what to listen for in opera, what the jargon means, and how opera has changed over the years. There is also information about going to the opera and what happens behind the scenes – some people may think that this breaks the illusion that opera creates, but others find the 'mechanics' of opera as fascinating as the art form itself.

No book can replace personal experience. You need to see opera live in a theatre to understand how a performance can take over your senses and shake your emotions to the core. After you have read this book you will have a better idea of which operas might appeal to you. The 12 featured operas described during the course of the book are among the most famous of all operas, and illustrate many of the different periods and styles of opera. These can then form the starting point for a lifetime's exploration of this wonderful art form.

Video clips

Videos clips from a number of operas have been chosen to accompany this book. These are highlighted in the text by the symbol .

A playlist of links to these videos can be found at **www.rhinegoldeducation.co.uk/myaccount**: please register and enter the code 36930U to access the playlist. You only need to register and use the code once: when revisiting the site just log in to go back to the playlist. There is also a playlist at www.youtube.com/user/RhinegoldEducation, although a few of the video clips chosen are only found on other websites.

The links were correct at the time of going to press but could be moved or deleted in future. If this happens please try a search for the piece of music concerned.

Dates

Dates indicate the year when an opera was first performed, unless stated otherwise.

Acknowledgements

The author wishes to thank Kieron Docherty, John McMurray and, in particular, Teresa Deacon of English National Opera for their help in the preparation of this book.

1. WHAT IS OPERA?

An **opera** is a type of drama in which singing has a central role in telling the story. Operas are usually performed on stage with singers in costume accompanied by an orchestra that is largely hidden from the audience. In addition to solo singers, there is often a chorus of voices that sing together, and many operas include dancing and sometimes elaborate spectacle. Most operas are sung throughout, but some include sections of spoken dialogue between the musical items.

All of these features can also be found in musicals – indeed, some opera companies occasionally stage musicals – but there are some important differences:

- Opera seldom includes the pop- or rock-based styles heard in musicals

- Opera requires singers with powerful voices that can be heard above the sound of a large orchestra in a big theatre, while musicals use singers who generally need amplification in order to be heard, and for that reason …

- Opera employs professional singers who can act, while musicals use professional actors who can sing with the aid of a microphone.

While the essence of opera is drama, soloists with a superb range of vocal skills are also required. Audiences are therefore attracted by the opportunity to hear some of the greatest singers in the world performing live. They are thrilled by successions of seemingly impossible high notes, almost unbelievable breath control, beauty of tone, speed of delivery, and so on – just as people are attracted to events such as the Olympics in order to see athletes run, row or swim faster, jump higher or throw further than seems humanly possible. And, as in sport, the most famous singers attract their own 'cult following' of supporters.

Most operas tell stories of love, hate, anger, passion, jealousy, heroism, a struggle for power, the cruelty of fate and other human conditions that we can all relate to in different ways. There is also a good deal of humanity and often comedy, although opera doesn't try to reflect real life in the way that a TV drama might. It couldn't possibly do so with all that singing! But the music serves to intensify the drama, sometimes seeming to make words unnecessary, and this is one of the main reasons for the continuing appeal of opera throughout more than four centuries.

Although some companies produce all operas in English, others present works in their original language, usually Italian, German or French. This is because even the best translations rarely manage to match every subtlety of the original language, especially where composers want particular vowel sounds to match specific notes in a song. Nowadays, opera in a foreign language is nowhere near as alarming as it might seem because a translation is projected on a display above the stage, synchronised to the words being sung.

Strange though it may seem, opera partly came about as the result of a mistake. Various intellectuals in late-16th century Italy became convinced that the plays of ancient Greece and Rome (written up to 2000 years earlier), must have been sung throughout in order for them to have had the great emotional impact on audiences that was reported at the time. Although that now seems unlikely, this belief led to new works that aimed to recreate this mythical classical drama, although using musical styles current around 1600.

These works were described at the time by various Italian phrases meaning 'fable in music', 'tragedy in music' or 'comedy in music'. By the late-17th century, the more general description *opera in musica* started to be used in Italy, which means 'works (or labours) in music' – perhaps reflecting the vast toil required in creating an opera. The abbreviation 'opera' soon became common in western Europe. Opera gradually moved away from its ancient classical roots, but the key element identified more than 400 years ago has remained ever since: the enormous potential offered by music to increase the impact of drama.

Of course, opera is entirely artificial – who conducts a conversation in song or sings to the world about their emotions? Opera strongly depends on the effect in drama called 'suspension of disbelief', in which members of the audience become so involved that they subconsciously ignore the real world. You might have experienced this for yourself. For example, when watching a good science-fiction film on the television, it is easy to forget that humans cannot really travel faster than the speed of light. You probably even put aside the fact that you are just watching actors from a box of electronics in the corner of the room. The experience with opera is similar, except that the people creating an operatic illusion for you are real – they are there before your eyes and not appearing on a screen or singing out of a loudspeaker.

So why is opera not more popular? In fact, opera is so popular that it is sometimes difficult to buy tickets unless booking months in advance. In addition, many people who have never been to see an opera enjoy the famous melodies from operas that have been used in television advertising and on film soundtracks. Opera singers have performed at major sporting events, 'Nessun dorma' from Puccini's opera *Turandot* became a football anthem and reached number two in the UK pop charts, and the crossover style of 'popera' (pop songs sung in an operatic style and operatic excerpts given a pop treatment) has a strong following.

However, tuneful excerpts stripped of their theatrical context are no more like opera than watching the five best goals of the season on a 'football highlights' feature. To experience the real thing, you need to see a good production delivered live on stage. The next section offers practical advice on doing just that.

Going to the opera

Britain has never had the large number of professional opera companies enjoyed by countries such as Germany and more recently the USA (where there are 125 opera houses). However, the five main opera companies in the UK are:

The Royal Opera	Royal Opera House, Covent Garden, London	www.roh.org.uk
English National Opera	The London Coliseum, St Martin's Lane, London	www.eno.org
Opera North	Grand Theatre, Leeds	www.operanorth.co.uk
Welsh National Opera	Wales Millennium Centre, Cardiff	www.wno.org.uk
Scottish Opera	Theatre Royal, Glasgow	www.scottishopera.org.uk

In London, The Royal Opera (which shares its venue with the Royal Ballet) produces operas in their original language, often with world-famous singers, while the nearby English National Opera specialises in producing operas in English. The three regional companies take productions on tour to other towns and cities as well as staging them at their headquarters venues.

There are other companies that perform for just a short season, often called an opera festival. The most famous is the Glyndebourne Festival, which is held at a purpose-built modern opera house in East Sussex for 14 weeks each summer. It is situated in the grounds of a country mansion and for that reason such festivals are sometimes known as 'Country House Opera'. Glyndebourne also runs a touring company (www.glyndebourne.com/glyndebourne-touring-opera), which takes opera on tour (mainly around the south of England) each autumn. The largest of the touring companies is English Touring Opera (www.englishtouringopera.org.uk), which gives up to 110 performances a year, often in theatres that would not normally host opera

There are also several 'pro-am' companies in which professional soloists are joined by an amateur chorus for certain specific productions.

All opera companies have websites on which you can book tickets, and some show the view available from different categories of seats. You can also book tickets by telephone or by visiting the opera house before the performance you wish to see. You can also use the opera companies' websites to research what discounts might be available for different types of bookings. These can include reduced prices for that day's performance ('stand-by tickets'), discounts for booking several different shows ('subscription tickets'), and reductions for 'group bookings'. Some companies offer substantial discounts for young people, such as English National Opera's *Access All Arias* scheme for those in the 16–30 age range.

If you have not been to an opera before, you are likely to enjoy it more if you choose a popular work (such as one of the 12 featured operas in this book). Good reviews in the press can also be a recommendation. Tickets can be expensive, and sometimes sell out long before the performances take place so it is worth making your visit to an opera special by booking tickets well in advance and aiming for the best seats you can reasonably afford.

Just as it helps to know the basic rules of the game when going to a football match, so it's worth reading up in advance about any opera you go to see. A summary of the plot of an opera (called the synopsis) is easy to find on the internet, as well as in books. It will also be included in the programme that you can purchase when you arrive. However, unless you particularly want a souvenir of the occasion, this is not an essential expense and you can usually ask instead for a free 'cast list' which gives the names of the performers.

People rarely dress up for opera these days – they just wear their normal clothes. However, because quite a lot of the audience arrive straight from work, you are as likely to see people in suits as in jeans. The only 'dress code' still common at opera performances in Britain is during the Glyndebourne Festival (although not including Glyndebourne touring performances) and at some other country house venues, where most men follow the tradition of wearing evening dress ('black tie') and women wear formal (often full length) evening gowns.

Aim to arrive in good time, as you may not be allowed to take your seat until the interval if you arrive late, which can be a huge disappointment. If you arrive early, most opera houses have bars where you can not only purchase drinks but also pre-order refreshments for the interval(s), thus saving queuing later in the evening. Many of the larger opera houses also have restaurants for those wishing to have a meal before the start of the performance. They all have cloakrooms where coats and bags can be left (sometimes for a small charge).

Be certain to turn off your mobile phone before you take your seat, and note that it is forbidden to take photographs or videos of the performance.

People usually applaud when the conductor enters to begin the performance, and again just before the start of the final act (when the orchestra often stands to acknowledge the applause). There is also usually applause at the end of each act of an opera (as the curtain comes down) and also after any particularly famous solos. At the end of the performance, there is generally a lot of applause and cheering during the **curtain call**. Just follow everyone else when it comes to applauding – and don't be surprised if there is a long, appreciative silence at the end of some operas, before the spell is broken and everyone starts clapping.

In short, going to an opera is no more complicated than going to a professional football match for the first time. Pay what you can afford (but expect to pay a lot for the best seats), wear what you want and follow everyone else when it comes to matters such as knowing when to cheer!

Finally, most professional opera companies display the words as they are sung on a screen above the stage and sometimes to individual seats. These **surtitles** are useful if the opera is sung in a foreign language, although they are now used even for works sung in English. If you do get lost in an opera, remember that just concentrating on the music can sometimes tell you as much about the drama as the actual words.

Most operas are divided into two or more main sections, each of which is called an **act**. Shorter works often have just two acts, separated by an interval (or intermission) of about 20 minutes, and usually last for about two and a half hours. Longer works are generally presented in three acts, often with two intervals, and typically last about, or a little over, three hours in all.

Many people choose to stretch their legs during the interval, and perhaps visit the bar or toilets. But it is fine to stay in your seat if you prefer.

Beyond that, it is difficult to generalise about what you might hear in any particular opera, although many include some or all of the following features:

- An **overture** is played by the orchestra before the curtain rises for the first time. It often sets the mood of the opera that follows, sometimes by quoting tunes that the audience will later hear sung. A short overture is sometimes called a **prelude**. There may be a break for applause after the overture, but some operas continue straight into the first act without any pause. In some operas, one or more of the later acts may be preceded by a short piece of orchestral music called an

intermezzo or **entr'acte**, originally composed to allow the scenery to be changed and so played while the curtain remains down.

- Each of the main characters is likely to have at least one substantial solo song (called an **aria** in more traditional operas). Arias tend to be quite reflective and so, when the dramatic pace quickens afterwards, there is likely to be rapid dialogue between characters (which may be spoken in some types of opera, although it is more usual for it to be sung). The soloists are also likely to sing together in **duets** and perhaps in larger **ensembles** such as **trios** and **quartets.**

- Many operas include a part for a **chorus** of singers, who may be required to take the role of courtiers, soldiers, villagers, church-goers and other people in crowd scenes. Some operas also include parts for a children's chorus.

- Solos, ensembles and chorus singing may sometimes follow each other in quick succession in a section known as a **scena** ('scene'). If this occurs at the end of an act, it is usually called a **finale** (for example, 'act one finale', 'act two finale' and so on).

- Some operas, particularly those written for the French stage in the 19th century, include a short **ballet** sequence, for which professional dancers are used.

- Some productions may make use of **supernumeraries** (or 'extras') such as non-singing actors to fill out the numbers in processions, or specialist performers, such as acrobats or puppeteers required for particular productions.

What you can expect in any successful production is the intensity that comes from hundreds of experts working together for months for your evening of enjoyment; the thrill of a large group of professional musicians performing without amplification only yards from your seat; the power of opera to bring together drama, music and the visual arts in the magic of a darkened theatre; the enjoyment of several hours of music cast as a unified whole; and the excitement of witnessing virtuoso singers at work, rather like having a front seat at the Olympics. These are just a few of the reasons why opera has remained popular for more than four centuries.

2. BEHIND THE SCENES

Opera houses

An opera house is simply a large theatre designed or adapted for opera, but it differs from most theatres in three important ways:

- There needs to be a large sunken area, known as the **orchestra pit,** between the stage and the front row of seats in order to accommodate an orchestra of at least 65 – 80 musicians. The pit is largely hidden from the audience and usually occupies the full width of the theatre as well as extending below the stage (see the plan *overleaf*).

- Because many operas include a chorus of at least 48 – 60 singers, as well as soloists and sometimes dancers and actors as well, extensive back-stage facilities are needed for large numbers of performers to change, apply make-up and warm up.

- Since the physical demands of singing without amplification in a large theatre mean that solo singers cannot perform eight shows a week, as many actors do, the larger opera houses run a system known as **repertory opera.** This involves alternating two or three different operas during the course of a week and means that the opera house must have the room to store, and the staff to move, scenery, costumes and other items needed for a different production each night, as well as for any new productions that are being rehearsed during the day.

The main parts of a medium-sized opera house are shown in the cross-section overleaf. The area shaded in pink is called the **front of house,** and is the part of the theatre used by the audience when they are not actually watching the production. It includes the **box office** (where tickets can be purchased), bars, cloakrooms, toilets and often a small restaurant.

The front of house also includes the **auditorium** (shaded yellow), where the audience sit for the performance. The seats at floor level are usually called the **stalls** and above these come the **dress circle, upper circle** and **balcony** – these names vary in different opera houses, but seats that are more distant from the stage are generally cheaper than those that have a good, unrestricted view.

Older opera houses have **boxes** that slightly project from the side walls of the auditorium, each of which contains seats for typically between two and 12 people. These are usually the most expensive seats of all, despite the fact that they rarely give a good view of the entire stage. Boxes are a remnant of the days when wealthy members of the audience valued *being seen* at the opera by others.

Apart from the stage itself, the area shaded in blue is known as **backstage** and is out of sight of the audience. It includes places to store and maintain the scenery, costumes and other items needed for several operas, as well as dressing rooms for performers and spaces for the lighting crew and stage management team.

Virtual tour of the Royal Opera House

The front of the stage is separated from the auditorium by the **proscenium**, behind which a safety curtain (often made of iron, and known as 'the iron') can be lowered to create a fire break in an emergency. Then come the house curtains, which close off the stage from the audience, although they are not used in all productions.

One of the most notable features in the cross-section is the **fly tower**. This rises to more than twice the height of the stage, allowing scenery to be 'flown' (raised out of sight of the audience) until it is required, as well as offering space for hidden lighting and special effects such as snow machines above the stage. Occasionally performers may be lowered on wires from the flies.

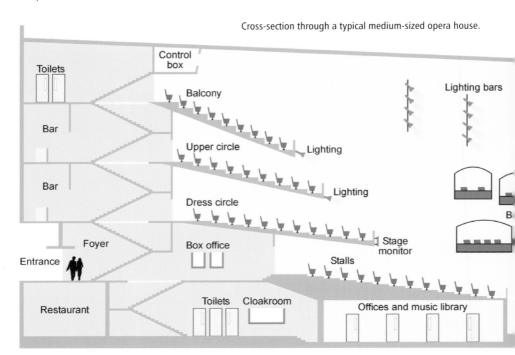

Cross-section through a typical medium-sized opera house.

At the rear of the stage there is often a backdrop or sky cloth, to help create the illusion of depth, and at the sides of the stage painted **flats** mask the **wings**, which are hidden areas from which performers move onto the stage. The angle of the stage can be raked so that the rear is higher (or occasionally lower) than the front. The scale of these items is usually impressive. For example, at the London Coliseum (the home of English National Opera) a typical backcloth is similar to the size of a large cinema screen at nine metres high and 16 metres wide. In recent years, video projection, onto the backcloth or onto semi-transparent gauzes nearer the front of the stage, has become another important element in some productions.

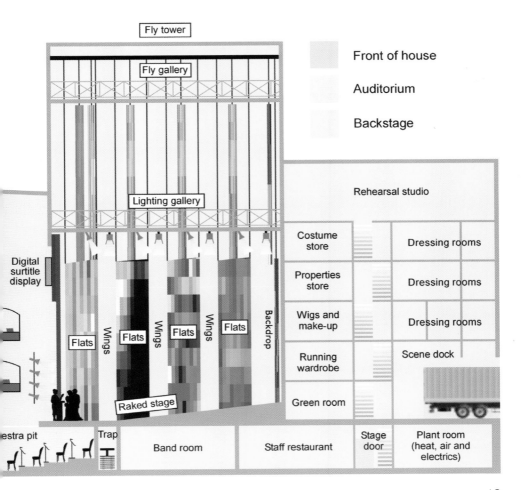

The stalls and orchestra pit at The London Coliseum, home of English National Opera

The collection of components that form the visual aspect of any one scene (known as 'the set') often includes raised platforms on which singers may need to perform, and three-dimensional constructions that can be as large as a small house. These items are often mounted on mobile platforms known as 'wagons' or 'trucks' that can be moved by silent hydraulic motors or by stage hands. In some cases, a designer will decide on a single set that can be rotated to afford different views to the audience (Adina's Diner pictured on page 77 is part of a rotating set).

In large modern venues, such as the Royal Opera House, Covent Garden (rebuilt in the late 1990s) it is possible to erect complete sets out of sight of the audience and out of the way of performers, on linked trucks that can quickly be moved on and off stage under computer control.

Opera houses in major cities are often large. The two main venues for opera in London are The London Coliseum (home of English National Opera), which is the largest theatre in the capital with 2359 seats, and the Royal Opera House in Covent Garden

Time-lapse of set changes at the Royal Opera House

(home of the Royal Opera and Royal Ballet) with 2268 seats. Both are dwarfed by the 3800 seats of the Metropolitan Opera House in New York City.

Despite this, most of the larger professional opera companies do not have room on site for all of their activities. They need warehouses in which scenery, costumes and other items can be stored until needed for **revivals** of productions in future years. They also need studios in which musicians can rehearse when the theatre itself is occupied by other productions. Some opera companies maintain their own workshops in which costumes and scenery are specially made for each production, although others now outsource this type of work to specialist theatrical supply companies.

Rehearsals

Rehearsals generally begin with the principal solo singers who, having learnt their parts at home, will have a number of coaching sessions with the conductor and a **répétiteur** (a pianist who plays the accompaniment). Soloists who are not singing in their own language will also often receive training from a language coach.

Rehearsals then move to a studio in which the sets will be mocked up as closely as possible. Singers may wear rehearsal clothes made to match the shape and weight of the costumes they will wear on stage, and will also practise with any items they are required to handle, such as wine glasses or lanterns. These are known as **props** (short for theatrical properties). The director of the production will teach each singer where and how to move in relation to the set and to other performers – a process

Members of the chorus of English National Opera in a music rehearsal

known as **blocking** – and specialist training will be provided for soloists involved in fight scenes or who need to use firearms in the show. A member of the stage management team usually attends these rehearsals to note where props and movable items, such as chairs and tables, need to be positioned on stage.

Members of the chorus start learning their parts under the guidance of the company's chorus master, who will have studied with the conductor to agree how the music should be interpreted. They, too, are accompanied by a *répétiteur*. Meanwhile the orchestra has its own rehearsals with the conductor. Before moving into the opera house, singers and orchestra come together for a **sitzprobe** (seated rehearsal).

A week or two before the first night, rehearsals move into the opera house, needing to finish in time on most days for all the scenery to be changed for the opera being performed to the public that evening. Rehearsals on stage involve working in costume, with most of the scenery in position. In addition, technical rehearsals take place to finalise lighting and scene changes. In some operas, stage hands are able to change sets while the house curtain is down between acts, but in others they may need to appear briefly on stage, either dressed in black or sometimes in costume.

Additional singers may be used to supplement the chorus, and non-singing actors, dancers, specialists such as jugglers and acrobats, and sometimes a children's choir may be required. Dancers will already have had their own demanding rehearsals with **choreographers**, as in the video clip where martial arts specialists and contemporary dancers are training for their roles in Verdi's *Aida*.

Verdi's *Aida*: rehearsing martial arts and contemporary dance sequences

Some rehearsals are still accompanied by a pianist, but there will usually be at least a couple of rehearsals on stage that are accompanied by the orchestra. Everything comes together for the **dress rehearsal** (known at Covent Garden as the general rehearsal), which aims to provide a complete run-through of the opera, often in front of an audience of staff and friends.

The opening night, usually a few days later, is described as the **premiere** if it is the first performance of a new work. The opera is then likely to be staged several times a week over several weeks in any one season, alternating with other works on the intervening evenings.

The repertory system operated by opera houses results in a great deal of activity, often at dead of night. After a performance has finished, the stage crew begin a change-over in which scenery for the opera that has just been presented is removed from the stage (a process known as 'striking the set'). Scenery and lighting for the next opera is

A *sitzprobe* (seated rehearsal) for English National Opera's world premiere of *Two Boys* by Nico Muhly (see page 181) at the Henry Wood Hall, London in 2011

A studio mock-up of a set for a rehearsal of *The Marriage of Figaro* by Mozart (English National Opera)

then moved into place. This may be for a stage rehearsal of some future production to take place the next morning, in which case another changeover will be needed in the afternoon to prepare the stage for the opera to be performed that evening.

Few opera houses have room to store scenery for more than two or three operas at a time, and so changeovers often involve the use of huge articulated lorries to transport sets of scenery and costumes between the theatre and the company's workshops and warehouses.

Moving sets

In fact, storing scenery can be one of the most limiting factors when planning a season of opera performances, as restricted space in many theatres often means that an opera that requires many different sets of scenery can only be rehearsed and performed alongside works that require a small number of simple sets.

Planning and production

Deciding which operas are to be produced, including the commissioning of new works, is usually the responsibility of several senior personnel:

- The chief executive (or managing director) responsible to a board of trustees for the management of the entire opera company

- The director of opera (or artistic director), responsible for the overall planning of new productions and revivals of past productions

Opera on the move

- The music director, who advises on all matters directly related to music and who is also usually the company's chief conductor

- The director of casting, who advises on the best singers to engage, including any rising talents that are starting to attract attention.

They and their staff will plan an opera season of up to a year in length that generally includes:

- revivals of productions that have been successful in previous years, that is, using the same scenery, costumes, lighting designs, etc.

- new productions of well-known operas

- a small number of works to be staged for the first time.

Almost all companies depend for a significant part of their box office receipts on the popularity of around 80 frequently performed operas. Although the precise works vary a little from one company to another, these pieces are often described as the 'standard repertoire'.

Many companies engage freelance staff to design and direct new productions of the standard repertoire, while the task of refreshing revivals of productions from previous seasons is usually given to an in-house team who work from detailed records kept of the original production. Revivals can sometimes continue for many years – even decades if the production has proved to be exceptionally popular.

Most opera houses engage specific singers on short contracts for important solo roles, and the need to work around their availability, as well as that of conductors, directors and designers, all of whom will have commitments with other companies, needs considerable advance planning. This, as well as the intricate task of allocating staff time and rehearsal spaces, co-ordinating the production of scenery, costumes and props, arranging transport for sets, and timetabling rehearsals for soloists, chorus, orchestra and technical staff, falls to the planning department. As well as working around the need to set up the stage before public performances on most evenings of the week, they have to dovetail similar sets of arrangements for a number of different operas, all in simultaneous but different stages of preparation. Once a master schedule has been prepared, details are circulated to all departments and staff involved. The implications of anything needing to be changed can have huge knock-on consequences.

A commission for an entirely new opera needs even longer advance planning. It usually begins by securing appropriate finance, which (like new productions of the standard repertoire) may come from one or more private sponsors, or it may be met by opera houses in different countries pooling their resources to underwrite the initial costs. These can be considerable, as a full-length opera can easily take more than a year to write, during which its creators need some source of income to survive. Once the full score has been written, and before rehearsals can start, parts in music notation have to be produced for each of the different instruments in the orchestra and scores have to be made from which singers can rehearse and *répétiteurs* can play.

The starting point for an opera is the **libretto** (Italian for 'little book'). It lists the characters, identifies the settings, and contains the words, thus outlining the dramatic structure of the work. Some composers have written their own libretti, and many have worked closely with their librettists, often asking for words to be re-written to fit particular musical ideas that they have already developed.

Some libretti tell an entirely original story, but in most cases the libretto is based on existing material, such as a legend, a shortened version of a play or novel, or an important historical event. Whatever the case, a successful librettist needs to be aware that while music can enhance the emotional content of the story, it will usually slow down the action, so he or she needs considerable skill in identifying the real essence of a drama and condensing this into a relatively small number of pages.

Nowadays, once the funding is in place for a new opera, an opera house will often bring together a librettist, composer, director and designer, so that they can work together on the creation of the work from the outset.

Composers vary in the way they go about writing opera. None today can match the sheer facility of Handel, Mozart or Rossini, each of whom could complete a three-hour opera in a matter of weeks. Composing a modern opera tends to be a long and reflective activity, often taking many months or even years. For example, Benjamin Britten, who preferred to work out ideas in his head, often while out walking, and later committing them to paper at his desk, spent more than a year of intensive work on his score for *Peter Grimes* (see page 164). Today, many composers use computer software to simulate the sounds and textures they are creating, but technology is no substitute for the human voice and usually some of the main sections of an opera will be tried out with soloists before the score is completed, especially if the music is being written with particular singers in mind.

The composer and librettist will also usually work with the opera's director from an early stage. The director is responsible for the artistic interpretation of the opera and its staging, either for a new work or a new production of an existing opera. The director oversees a large creative team and works with the singers, after they have learnt their music, to provide insights into how they should act their roles. This involves matters such as how and where they should move, and also how they should react

The cutting table in the costume workshop (English National Opera)

to each other and to the unfolding drama, in order to bring the production to life as a coherent whole.

The role of the designer is crucial in determining the visual impact of the work. When Benjamin Britten was composing *Peter Grimes* he asked the designer, Kenneth Green, to provide preliminary sketches of the scenery to help him visualise the work that he was composing. In addition to sketches and drawings, designers generally use a model box, in which miniature versions of sets can be evaluated in three dimensions. Designers may also be responsible for costume designs, although sometimes specialist costume designers are used.

Styles of opera design have changed dramatically over the years. Kenneth Green's sets for the first production of *Peter Grimes* in 1945 were very naturalistic, with fishermens' cottages, a church and an inn clustered around the seafront. In contrast, John Macfarlane's austere designs for the 2011 production of the work at Covent Garden reflected its bleak East Anglian landscapes through expanses of muted colour, minimal detail and atmospheric lighting. The 2009 production of *Peter Grimes* at English National Opera adopted yet another design decision, by changing the period in which the work is set from the early 19th century (when the poem on which it is based was written) to war-torn 1945, the year in which the opera was composed. Such changes of period, which have become increasingly common in recent decades, can often cast new light on familiar works.

Once set and costume designs have been approved, they may be sent out to be constructed by independent theatrical suppliers, although the largest opera companies maintain their own workshops for this purpose. Considerable trouble is taken to ensure that the results will be effective under theatrical lighting, including dyeing cloth and mixing paints to match colour swatches provided by the designer.

Costume design requires a team of buyers, dyers, cutters, seamstresses and tailors, all with a good knowledge of the history of costume, as they may be called upon to produce authentic-looking clothes for any period. They also have to be aware of the needs of singers. For example, tight corsetry for a 19th-century costume can impede a singer's breathing, while for a medieval character a long wig or a helmet that covers the ears can make it difficult for a singer to hear other performers.

Whether or not costumes are made in-house, the theatre needs a team known as the running wardrobe, who are responsible for the final fitting of clothes and shoes, as well as cleaning, ironing and storing them after use, and carrying out minor repairs as needed. With up to 100 performers on stage in some works, and with several operas running simultaneously, this is a very considerable task. Allied to their work is that of the dressers, who assist singers in putting on more complex costumes, the props master, in charge of the many items the cast may use on stage, and the wigs department, who have to be prepared to deal with anything from ancient Egyptian hairstyles to punk mohican cuts in vivid colours.

Wigs and make-up

Set construction requires teams of carpenters, welders and scene painters. Sets may be used for 20 years or more, and safety is paramount when scenery includes steps, ladders, balconies, sloping floors and trucked pieces that will move on stage. There are also

Set building and painting

many practical considerations, such as ensuring that items are not too large to store in the wings or too heavy to be flown from above the stage. As with costumes, some in-house staff are needed in the theatre to carry out minor repairs.

Co-ordinating the work of all these teams is the job of the production manager, who has to ensure that every aspect of the show stays on schedule and within budget. This includes the work of the lighting team, who play an important part in creating the atmosphere of an opera and who have to ensure that the cast are adequately and appropriately illuminated. The large stages of opera houses require hundreds of lamp fixtures, as well as occasional special effects such as lightning. A lighting designer creates a plan, first using models of the sets, which is then put together by the chief electrician. Modern fixtures allow the angle, colour, size and shape of the beam in individual lanterns to be controlled from a computerised lighting console, which can memorise the correct speed and sequence of changes for each opera.

Dressing wigs at the Coliseum, home of English National Opera

23

Performances of an opera are under the control of a stage manager, who usually has a team of assistants. The stage manager works from a desk in the wings on one side of the stage, known as the prompt corner, using a carefully annotated score of the music. He or she is responsible for ensuring that announcements are made to the audience and performers when the performance is soon to begin, notifying the front of house staff when to close the doors, cueing the conductor to enter the pit, followed by reminding the lighting desk to dim the house lights in the auditorium. During the show, the stage manager checks that performers are ready for their entrances, cues the stage crew for scene changes and the lighting desk for light changes, ensures that the fly crew know when to raise and lower the main curtains (known as the tabs) and any pieces of scenery that have to be flown, and ensures that any special effects, such as video projections or pyrotechnics, begin at precisely the right moment.

The stage manager controlling a performance of Wagner's 'The Ride of the Valkyries'

The front of house manager is responsible for a large team. Box office staff who sell tickets, either in person or by telephone or via the internet, are usually full time employees, but cleaners, ushers, programme sellers, bar staff, cloakroom attendants, tour guides and caterers are generally part-time workers.

Of course, the music department is central to the work of any opera house. Headed by the music director (usually the chief conductor), there are a number of staff involved in the day-to-day administration and running of the department. The music librarian's team, who look after all the scores and orchestral parts for the operas in the company's repertoire, are also often responsible for the surtitle screens. These have to be manually co-ordinated, very precisely timed to the performance as it is being sung.

The orchestra manager and assistant typically work with a permanent orchestra of some 60 players, although this number may be considerably increased by freelance

High above the stage in the flies, a flyman can easily raise and lower large items that are balanced by counterweights players engaged for specific large-scale operas. The frequent need for the orchestra to rehearse in venues away from the opera house means that there may be a logistics manager to assist with transporting large instruments, sheet music and so forth.

A permanent chorus of between 40 and 60 voices is trained by a chorus master and assistant, and there will usually be a chorus manager to deal with the administration of this team. As with the orchestra, the size of the chorus may be increased by engaging freelance singers for some works. Freelance singers are also usually engaged for solo roles, although members of the chorus may be allocated minor parts, and *répétiteurs* are employed to provide piano accompaniments for the singers.

Like any large organisation, an opera company needs a number of departments to promote its work and service the needs of its employees. These typically include:

- **Development:** fundraising by attracting sponsors, producing recordings, videos and other merchandise for sale, raising money through special events and back-stage tours, running a society of 'friends' of the opera house who provide regular support, and so on.

- **Marketing:** production of brochures, programmes, advertising in the press, in the locality, on websites and often overseas, public relations, running mailing lists and liaising with the media through a press office, including the organisation of podcasts for publicity, photographs for press reviews and so on.

- **Personnel:** dealing with recruitment, contracts, engagement of freelance extras for specific productions, liaison with schools, licensing authorities and chaperones when children are required to perform in an opera.

- **Facilities:** responsible for the upkeep of the premises and the hire to others of rooms, equipment, scenery, costumes or entire productions.

- **Education:** arranging events and courses for schools and colleges, and for organising community outreach projects.

- **Finance:** financial controller, accountants, bookkeepers, pay clerks, budget forecast staff and so on.

As well as giving an indication of the wide variety of jobs in an opera house and the enormous amount of work that goes into presenting a production, this short overview also reveals why opera is a costly business, with large companies employing many hundreds of staff. As the 17th-century French playwright Molière once observed, 'Of all the noises known to man, opera is the most expensive'.

Even though the best opera tickets can match, and even exceed, the cost of those for premier league football matches, opera companies have almost always depended on additional income. In the past, this was provided by wealthy aristocrats who saw lavish support for the arts as a way of bolstering their own status (although many also happened to enjoy opera).

Today, the shortfall is provided by a combination of government grants and private sponsorship, the latter ranging from small amounts given by keen opera-goers to generous amounts donated by wealthy individuals, trusts and corporations who wish to be associated with opera.

Operatic voices

Singers and the roles they play are categorised by their vocal ranges. In the chorus the main sections are as follows (from highest to lowest, with the two types of female voice listed before the two types of male voice):

- Sopranos
- Altos (sometimes called contraltos)
- Tenors
- Basses

When a composer wants a thicker choral sound, these parts may be divided into first and second sopranos, first and second altos, and so on, resulting in eight parts rather than four.

The main soloists in an opera are generally known as the principals. Traditionally, the leading female singer used to be called the *prima donna* (first lady) and any celebrated female singer was known as a *diva* (goddess). These terms have more generally become associated with vain or temperamental people and, like *primo uomo* (first man), are rarely used in opera today outside Italy.

Soloists usually categorise their type of voice more specifically than chorus singers, although not all limit themselves to roles of a single type, and many singers' voices change over the course of their careers. Some of the more common types are:

Coloratura soprano	A very high soprano with a light quality that is suited to singing florid passages of music known as *coloratura*
Lyric soprano	A warm voice with a bright, full sound
Dramatic soprano	A powerful, more darkly coloured soprano voice
Mezzo soprano	Often the lowest type of female voice for soloists, as solo parts for altos are rare
Light lyric tenor (or *leggero* tenor)	Like the coloratura soprano, a light and very high voice particularly suited to early 19th-century opera
Lyric tenor	A warm voice with a bright, full sound
Dramatic tenor	A more robust type of voice, often identified as the typical type of operatic tenor
Heldentenor ('Hero tenor')	A dark, weighty and powerful tenor voice, particularly associated with the operas of Wagner
Baritone	Midway in range between tenor and bass, baritone parts often need a dark voice with bite as well as a lyrical quality
Bass-baritone	A dramatic voice, slightly lower than a baritone, but that can manage a few notes above the normal bass range
Basso buffo	A flexible bass voice suited to comic roles
Basso profundo	The very lowest type of bass voice

Some operas include parts for children's voices, which are generally designated as treble (a similar range to soprano, although usually without any really high notes) and alto (never contralto).

One type of voice that has not been heard in opera houses for nearly two centuries is the **castrato**: an adult male with a soprano or alto range caused by emasculation before the age of puberty. Such a practice, which developed in 16th-century Italy, initially to replace boy singers in church music, rightly seems barbaric to us today. However, during the 100-year period in which *castrati* were popular in opera (from about 1675 onwards), the huge fame and financial rewards available to the best singers tempted a number of poor families to condemn their sons to this particular fate.

Casting *castrato* parts in modern performances of early opera is a problem, because they generally played male roles which often don't make musical sense if sung by a tenor or bass, an octave lower than written. One solution is to use a female singer in male clothing – a type of part known as a **breeches role** or '**trouser role**'. In fact, it became standard practice after the *castrato* fell from favour, to deliberately write for a woman in male clothing if there was a part for a young male teenager (who is usually falling in love for the first time). The potential confusion of trouser roles, which can be reduced to farce if the plot then calls for the woman dressed as a man to disguise herself as a woman, inevitably became the stock-in-trade for many a comic opera over the years.

The other solution for filling *castrato* roles today is to use a countertenor, a normal male voice that is extended to the top of the alto range by using *falsetto*, a technique that can be experienced by singing a high-pitched 'coo-ee' and that is occasionally used by some pop singers. Most countertenors have an alto range, but a few (sometimes known as sopranists) can manage the soprano roles once sung by *castrati*. The countertenor voice came back into favour in the second half of the 20th century, and since then a number of roles for solo countertenor have been created in contemporary opera.

The dome at The London Coliseum

3. THE ORIGINS OF OPERA

In western culture the period between about 1450 and 1600 is now known as the Renaissance. This word means 're-birth' and it refers to the renewed confidence in human achievement that developed as the poverty and mysticism of the middle ages gave way to an age of prosperity based on trade with newly-discovered lands. The invention of printing helped to create a more literate population, and greater wealth and education became the trigger for splendid new developments in the arts.

An important aspect of this re-birth was a new appreciation of the architecture, sculpture, literature and philosophy of ancient Greece and Rome that had been created some 1500 years earlier. In the city-states of Italy, where the Renaissance began, occasions such as royal weddings were often marked by the performance of plays by those ancient Romans, or modelled on their style. These could be heavy going, even for keen fans, and so a lighter **interlude** called an *intermedio* (an 'intermediate' piece) was often performed between the acts of these plays.

Intermedii weren't usually related to the plot of the main play, but they were very entertaining, with a lively mix of solo songs, group singing (in the form of madrigals), dancing and special scenic effects. Reports from the time suggest that the *intermedio* was often more interesting than the play that it interrupted!

Although *intermedii* were forerunners of opera, there are important differences. *Intermedii* were usually assembled from existing music by a variety of composers rather than being specially written. Also, while they often had a unifying theme (such as gods coming down from on high to bless a bridal couple, acted out in mime to a musical accompaniment) they rarely had a dramatic plot. Nevertheless some, such as those designed for the wedding of Ferdinando I de' Medici, Grand Duke of Tuscany, in 1589 were on a colossal scale and included dances, instrumental pieces and vocal ensembles (madrigals), as well as solo song.

To convey a dramatic story through song, an especially clear and simple style of vocal writing was needed – and this, too, developed out of the period's fascination with ancient culture. A group of intellectuals known as the Florentine Camerata (the comrades of Florence) convinced themselves – probably wrongly – that ancient Greek plays were sung throughout, using music to heighten the impact of the words. They had no idea how it might have sounded, but one of their number, Vincenzo

Galilei (father of Galileo, the famous astronomer), laid down some key principles in his 'Dialogue about Ancient and Modern Music', published in 1581:

■ For clarity, the text should be sung by a soloist with the simplest accompaniment.

■ The words must be declaimed naturally and without repetition, as they would be when spoken, avoiding the dance-like rhythms of popular songs.

■ The melody must reflect the feeling and emotion of the entire passage of text.

These ideas were put into practice by several members of the Camerata in the late 16th century. One was Giulio Caccini who wrote a number of pieces in the new style, which he eventually collected together and published in 1602. Caccini indicated their novelty by using the title *Le nuove musiche* (The new music).

Here is the opening of the fourth piece from the collection ('Love, I depart, and I feel in the parting a death'):

This type of vocal writing, which is more expressive than speech but less tuneful than song, was called **stile rappresentativo** (theatrical style) because it proved ideal for stage works in which singers need to deliver a lot of text fairly concisely.

Caccini's 'Love, I depart'

The texture seen in this example, in which a single vocal line is supported by an accompaniment simple enough to allow the singer to convey the words expressively, soon became known as **monody**.

However, the accompaniment is not quite as bare as it appears. Caccini used a recent invention called figured bass, in which chords are indicated in a type of shorthand. When there is no indication to the contrary, the musicians would play a triad on the bass note – G minor for the first four bass Gs above, followed by F major when the bass moves to F. Anything out of the ordinary was indicated by symbols below the bass part. For example, in the second bar, the 7 indicates that an expressive 7th (D) should be added to the chord of Eb major.

These harmonies would be improvised on one or more instruments that could play chords, such as a small pipe organ, harpsichord, harp or lute. The musicians were free to space the notes as they wished, and might improvise short melodic fragments in appropriate places. In addition, the bass line was usually reinforced by a low-pitched string instrument such as a cello or violone (a predecessor of the double bass).

This type of part was called the **basso continuo** (continuous bass) because it ran throughout the music; the musicians who play from the part are called the continuo players. It quickly became indispensable in almost all music for more than one performer, and its presence is one of the defining features of the baroque style.

Such was the wealth and musical interest in the courts of renaissance Italy that professionally trained singers became increasingly common from the 1570s onwards – indeed, Caccini, the composer of the example above, was renowned as a singer and singing teacher. Many of these soloists were in high demand for their virtuoso skills, which would soon be put to use in opera. Thus, some of the most important ingredients for the creation of the first operas were in place by 1600:

■ The *intermedio* as a model for stage works based on music

■ The monody as a way of setting longer sections of text to music, with a purely supportive accompaniment from a small group of continuo instruments

■ Professional singers who could deliver dramatic music expressively, as well as impress audiences with their performing skills.

4. BAROQUE OPERA (1600–1750)

The first work that might be recognised today as an opera was **Dafne**, composed mainly by Jacopo Peri and performed in Florence in 1598. Only the libretto and fragments of the score survive, but it is clear from these that Peri intended the music to intensify the drama, using the methods suggested by the Florentine Camerata. The plot was based on a Greek myth, and the work was sung throughout.

Only a small audience saw *Dafne*, but it was successful enough to be repeated in 1599 and 1600.

Peri's next opera, **Euridice**, survives intact. It was first staged in 1600, the year in which Caccini had composed his own version of

Centres of Baroque opera in Italy (map shows the boundaries of modern Italy)

the same story. Like *Dafne*, both versions of *Euridice* are fairly small scale, with a plot based on Greek myth. Much of the drama is conveyed through monody, varied by the inclusion of simple **strophic arias** (songs in which the same music is used for each verse) and choruses that were probably sung by five solo voices.

None of these early works are enticing enough to be regularly performed today, and opera might have disappeared as a failed experiment in reviving Greek drama had not the most famous composer of the age turned his talents to the stage.

Monteverdi

By 1592, Claudio Monteverdi (1565–1643) was working in northern Italy as a musician for the Duke of Mantua, a wealthy patron of the arts who also employed the famous painter Rubens at his court. Monteverdi's early publications were sets of madrigals composed in the renaissance style of the late 16th century. However, after 1600 he became increasingly involved in the new developments of the baroque style.

The Duke of Mantua had been in the audience (probably with Monteverdi) at the first performance of Peri's *Euridice* in Florence in 1600, and the duke resolved that his own staff should produce something similar but grander for the 1607 carnival in Mantua. The result was ***L'Orfeo***, which has a libretto by Alessandro Striggio (the duke's secretary) and music by Monteverdi (by now the duke's director of music). The work was described as a *favola in musica* (a fable in music) but would now be recognised as an opera. Indeed, it is the earliest opera that is regularly performed today.

As in most early operas, the story has its origins in ancient myth – in this case, the Greek legend of Orpheus and Eurydice as recounted by the Roman poets Virgil (in about 29 BC) and Ovid (in AD 8), although probably dating back much earlier.

It is the same legend that had formed the basis of the settings of *Euridice* by Peri and Caccini, and that would be the subject of operas by many later composers, not least because the hero of the story is a singer, and the plot outlines a vivid sequence of emotional events – love, tragedy, rescue and death – ideal for setting to music.

The Orpheus Myth

Orpheus is the greatest musician who ever lived. One strum on his lyre and all of nature gathers around to listen. He marries the beautiful Eurydice, but she is killed by a poisonous snake and her spirit sinks to the underworld. Orpheus is grief-stricken, but resolves to find her. He so charms the monsters of Hades with his singing that they agree to let Eurydice return to the human world on condition that Orpheus has no doubt that she is following him. He listens closely for her footsteps, but forgets that spirits make no sound and in his anxiety he turns to check that she is still there. He sees only a fleeting glimpse of Eurydice before she is lost to him for ever.

The tragic conclusion of the myth was a problem for the early composers of opera. Peri and Caccini both end their settings of *Euridice* with the lovers happily returning to the mortal world, while Monteverdi ends *L'Orfeo* with the hero being taken up to heaven by his father, the god Apollo. Monteverdi's version is also different in other ways, reflecting a considerably more ambitious concept:

- It is much longer, filling five acts and taking some two hours to perform
- While monody still plays an important role, Monteverdi draws on many types of music from the period to provide variety within this long time-span

33

■ The instrumental accompaniment is much more colourful and it is often directly related to the drama – Monteverdi specifies about 40 instruments in all, contrasting the combination of strings and recorders that depict the happiness of the lovers with dark trombones and the fierce buzzing sound of the regal (a keyboard instrument pumped by bellows) that represent the underworld, and using a harp and organ to accompany Orpheus the musician.

featured opera

L'Orfeo begins with a fanfare, based entirely on one chord and played three times, after which a brief prologue about the power of music introduces the drama to follow. It is punctuated by a short instrumental passage marked by Monteverdi as a **ritornello** (Italian for 'little return') which not only occurs six times in the prologue but also returns later in the opera, helping to unify the long work.

The marriage of Orpheus and Euydice is then celebrated in Act One, in a succession of joyful solos, duets, choruses and dances. The festivities continue into Act Two, where Orpheus contrasts his happiness with the emptiness he felt before meeting Eurydice. This is expressed in a strophic aria with a lively rhythm that reflects the type of light vocal music Monteverdi was writing at this time. It is just one of the many styles he drew upon when creating *L'Orfeo*:

This carefree music is also a dramatic device, designed to maximise the contrast with what happens next – the arrival of a messenger bringing news that Eurydice has died from a snake bite. Monteverdi

Monteverdi's *L'Orfeo*

sets the dialogue in a passage of intensely dramatic monody shown in the next music example.

The messenger attempts to break the news with *(a)*, 'Your beautiful Eurydice…', but Orpheus is so startled to hear her name that he interrupts with *(b)*, 'Oh no, what is it?', wrenching the music into an entirely unrelated key. Determined to complete the dreadful task, the messenger returns to her original key and melody for *(c)*, 'Your beloved wife… is dead'. At last, as the news sinks in, Orpheus completes the phrase with a cry of *(d)*, 'Alas!', before falling silent:

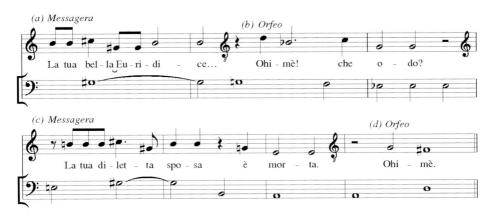

The central feature of Act Three (and of the entire opera) is Orpheus's aria 'Possente spirto' (Powerful spirit), which Monteverdi composed in strophic variation form – a set of variations on the music of the first verse, most of which are

Monteverdi's *L'Orfeo*, 'La tua bella Euridice'

punctuated by instrumental *ritornelli* (some with echo effects). When *L'Orfeo* was published in 1609 Monteverdi added an extra stave in the score to show how a virtuoso singer might lavishly embellish the basic notes of this song. Dramatically, the purpose of 'Possente spirto' is for Orpheus to demonstrate his skills as a singer in order to be allowed to cross the River Styx and enter the underworld to search for Eurydice.

The couple are reunited in Act Four, and Orpheus starts to lead his wife back to the mortal world in a lively strophic aria underpinned by the regular pace of a bass part in even rhythm, nowadays known as a 'walking bass'. However, after three verses he starts to have doubts and the steady

The title page of Monteverdi's *L'Orfeo*, published in Venice in 1609

35

tread of the walking bass ceases as he stops to listen for her footsteps. Threatening offstage voices remind us of what will happen if he looks back, but he does, and so sees Eurydice for only a moment before losing her for ever.

Act Five sees Orpheus lamenting his loss, with an offstage echo that seems to mock his very words. There is some uncertainty about the original ending, but in the first published score of 1609 the god Apollo arrives to chide Orpheus (his son) for being a slave to his emotions. Apollo then accompanies his son to the heavens in a cloud machine from where Orpheus can expect to see Eurydice in the stars.

L'Orfeo was performed twice in Mantua during 1607 and the score was published in 1609. There may have been productions in other cities over the next few decades, although this is not certain. After Monteverdi's death his music was largely forgotten until rediscovered by scholars some 250 years later. Today *L'Orfeo* is performed fairly frequently, often using replicas of instruments from Monteverdi's day.

Monteverdi's next opera, **L'Arianna**, followed in 1608 and was reported to have been a success but, apart from one song, the music was never published and is now lost. In 1613 Monteverdi moved some 80 miles east of Mantua to take charge of the music at St Mark's Venice, but he was to return to opera later in his life, as explained in the next section.

Meanwhile, as enthusiasm for opera spread to Rome and other Italian cities, it was realised that effective plots could be based on subjects other than ancient mythology. For instance, **La liberazione di Ruggiero** (1625) by Francesca Caccini (daughter of Giulio Caccini) was based on an episode about witchcraft and sorcery taken from an epic poem by Ariosto, written only a century earlier. It was also the first opera to be composed by a woman but, like all early operas, it was private entertainment, financed by aristocrats to demonstrate their wealth to courtiers and visitors, and not open to the public. That was soon to change once the citizens of Venice had fallen in love with opera.

Venetian opera

After Monteverdi arrived in Venice in 1613 he concentrated mainly on writing church music and publishing further sets of madrigals. The city had an elected leader, not an aristocratic ruling family, and so there was no tradition of lavish court entertainments like those in Florence and Mantua.

However, the merchant families who had created the wealth of Venice had an eye for commercial opportunities and realised the potential profit in opening theatres especially for opera. Such families could provide the financial backing, supported by others who would lease boxes in the theatre for long periods, while tickets for individual shows could be sold to the increasing number of visitors (particularly from Britain) for whom going to an opera in Venice would soon become one of the highlights on their grand tours of Italy.

The first such venture was the *Teatro San Cassiano*, opened by the Tron family in 1637. It was the first public opera house in the world and now anyone who could afford a ticket for the opera had access.

What started as an experiment soon became a roaring success. Eleven opera houses had opened in Venice by the end of the 17th century, with up to six operating simultaneously – all in a city with a population no larger than modern-day Hereford, although numbers were doubled by visitors during the carnival season.

Paying audiences changed the nature of opera because they used their patronage in this competitive market to express preferences for more comedy, more spectacle, a bit of sauciness, and the opportunity to hear their most favoured star singers.

Monteverdi, now in his seventies, eyed this development with interest. In 1640 he cautiously dipped a toe in the water with a revised version of his now lost *L'Arianna* for the opening of the *Teatro San Moisè*, Venice's third opera house. Its success spurred Monteverdi to compose three entirely new operas in his old age:

- *Il ritorno d'Ulisse in Patria* (The Return of Ulysses to his Homeland), 1640

- *Le nozze d'Enea con Lavinia* (The Marriage of Enea and Lavinia), 1641

- *L'incoronazione di Poppea* (The Coronation of Poppea), 1642/3

The music of the second of these works is now lost but *Poppea*, in particular, shows Monteverdi adapting his style to the needs of the new public opera houses. Much of their budgets were spent on attracting the best singers of the day and as a result, orchestras were tiny. Instruments are not specified in the score of *Poppea*, but the singers are accompanied by just a group of continuo instruments and it seems likely that the only other instruments involved were two violins.

In *Poppea* there is less reliance on monody, and more emphasis on melodic songs that give the singers opportunity for displays of vocal virtuosity. Tragic moments are relieved by comedy, including a dreadful old crone of a nurse (often played by a man

The Venetian Stage

The Venetians needed to attract the public to their new opera houses in order to make a profit. In addition to engaging star singers and including comic characters, copies of the opera libretto were on sale for those who wished to follow the words in the candlelit theatre. Most operas included special effects, ranging from instant scene transformations to machines that could mimic the sound of thunder or lower gods on clouds from the skies. The genius behind these devices was Giacomo Torelli (1608–1678), the most important set designer of his day.

The invention that most appealed to opera house owners was a system that enabled entire scenes to be changed by a single person, rather than the dozen or more stagehands previously needed. The principles are shown in the diagram *opposite*. The flats with painted trees are currently visible to the audience, while those with painted columns would be out of sight (in the diagram the main curtains are shown open wider than normal for clarity).

All of the flats are mounted on posts which pass through slots in the stage floor, supported by small wagons running on tracks under the stage. The wagons are attached to ropes wound around a central shaft or windlass. Also wound around this shaft is a rope (not shown in the diagram) that passes through a pulley mounted in the roof of the theatre. Just one person is needed to release a large stone counterweight attached to the far end of this control rope, which then turns the windlass, pulling the hidden flats into view and sliding the onstage flats off into the wings. Another rope attached to the windlass could raise and lower borders hung above the stage at the same time as the flats moved.

Once the flats were out of sight, painted canvases for later scenes could be attached to the frames and the counterweight raised to the roof, ready to repeat the entire process for the next scene change.

For simplicity, the diagram shows only two painted flats on each side of the stage. In practice, there would be up to eight per side, all capable of moving together, and each gradually staggered inwards to give the impression of a perspective receding into infinity. Audiences thought the effect so astonishing that Torelli became known as the 'great magician'.

A system of counterweights suspended from pulleys in the roof of the theatre was also used to fly scenery, while a pit at the back of the stage could be used for effects such as ships sailing through raging waves. Some of the most sophisticated machinery allowed singers to appear to ascend to the heavens, using a suspended chariot that could move from side to side above the stage before disappearing from view into the flies.

The Venetian scene-changing system

in drag) and a drunken singing competition between two shrill *castrati*. There's also quite a bit of lewdness, and the entire work focuses on the adulterous relationship between the Roman emperor Nero, and his mistress Poppea. In the final act, Nero divorces and exiles his wife, leaving Poppea to be crowned empress and the audience wondering if perhaps vice *can* triumph over virtue!

It is thought that some of the music for *Poppea* may have been contributed by other composers, particularly Monteverdi's pupil, Francesco Cavalli (1602–1676). He became the most important composer in Venice after Monteverdi's death in 1643, writing at least 30 operas (not all of which survive). One of the best known today is **La Calisto** (1651), based on the myth of an ancient Greek goddess, but produced in the new Venetian style.

It was at this time that orchestras started to become more standardised, based on strings and continuo, but with the occasional addition of wind instruments towards the end of the 17th century. The orchestra would typically play a **sinfonia** (which might now be described as an overture) at the start of the work, and would accompany some of the increasing number of solo arias, as well as playing *ritornelli* at various points.

By the 1650s, the slow-moving monody used in the earliest operas was falling out of fashion. Instead, composers set passages of dialogue as **recitative** (from the Italian *recitare*, meaning 'to recite'). This is a type of speech-like singing that developed from monody but which was usually faster and more lightly accompanied:

In this example, from Cavalli's **Serse** (1654), recitative is ideal for the rapid exchanges between Arsamene and his servant, who is about to deliver a love letter for his master ('Here's the letter, Elviro … Are you really sure? … My life depends upon it …').

A number of conventions developed in the performance of recitative. In order to allow the words to be heard clearly, the continuo accompaniment was often played by just a harpsichord or lute, and the chords were kept very short, despite the long notes in the bass part (which composers used to save writing many rests). The use of minimal accompaniment allowed singers to interpret their rhythms with a certain degree of expressive freedom and singers would also make small changes to the written pitches of some of their notes, particularly at the ends of phrases.

By its nature, recitative is rarely musically interesting – its purpose is to move the plot along without breaking the musical spell by dropping into spoken dialogue. For that reason, composers usually followed a recitative with a more melodic aria, in which a character would reflect on the situation they are in, leading to a conventional pairing of 'recitative and aria'. Whereas the most intense moments in the earliest operas were often set to monody, recitative was more utilitarian, and so the focus for passionate expression tended to shift to the aria.

One of the most popular types of aria in Venetian opera was the lament on a ground – a sad song, consisting of a succession of different vocal phrases written over a constantly repeated phrase in the bass (called a ground bass). The latter often took the form of a chromatic descent from tonic (the key note) to the dominant (the second most important note in a key), as in the following example from Cavalli's **Egisto** (1643). The four-bar bass is repeated 19 times in succession, creating an almost oppressively intense mood for this setting of 'Weep, sorrowful eyes, that cry with plaintive tears':

pian - to mi - o   pian - - - - ga,

Venetian opera reached its peak in the 1650s, although the city has continued to be an important centre for opera ever since. Venice's most famous composer in the early 18th century, Vivaldi, is thought to have written nearly 50 operas (although many of these have not survived), and a number of 19th- and 20th-century operas received their first performance at *La Fenice*, first opened in 1792, twice rebuilt, and now the main venue for opera in Venice.

Neapolitan opera

Most of the earliest operas to be heard in Naples, the principal city in southern Italy, were composed and performed by Venetians. One of the first, in 1651, may have been a revised version of Monteverdi's *Poppea*, composed some eight years earlier.

However, Naples was well placed to develop its own musical traditions as it had four large orphanages in which boys were trained for employment as musicians. These organisations were known as *conservatorii* because they 'conserved' or protected children. The word is still used today as a name for a music college, usually in its French form of *conservatoire*.

By the 1680s, an increasingly standardised type of opera was starting to develop in Naples, particularly in the hands of Alessandro Scarlatti (1660–1725). Known at the time as *dramma per musica* (drama through music), such works are now called **opera seria** (serious opera). They were to become the most important type of Italian opera for the next 100 years. Scarlatti wrote more than 60 operas, as well as a huge amount of other music, and perhaps due to the speed at which he had to compose, found it congenial to work to the type of template outlined on page 50.

Many of Scarlatti's operas begin with an overture in three sections (fast – slow – fast), now known as an **Italian overture**. The first section was a call to attention, the second was often just a short link, and the third was usually in a dance style of the day. The rest of the opera consisted of a long series of arias, mainly reflective in character, separated by recitatives in which the action was carried forward. There were often one or two duets for variety, but the role of the chorus diminished. This structure of self-contained pieces (or numbers) is known as a **number opera**.

The type of recitative illustrated at the top of page 40 became known as *recitativo secco* (dry recitative) because of its minimal accompaniment. A more elaborate type of recitative was often used for passages of high drama. Known as *recitativo accompagnato* (accompanied recitative), it has an orchestral accompaniment.

It was also at this time that composers began to prefer a three-part form for arias, in preference to earlier structures such as the strophic song and ground bass aria. An opening section was followed by a middle section on a complementary idea, after which the composer wrote the instruction *da capo* (from the 'top') indicating that the first section should be repeated. The result is a form that could be represented by the letters ABA, and this became known as a **da capo aria**. Again, the opportunity to use a two-word instruction to save many hours of composition and yet maintain aesthetic integrity, clearly appealed to the hard-pressed composers of the day.

Singers loved the *da capo aria* because, by convention, they could freely embellish the vocal line in the repeated section to show off their vocal skills. This decoration would often include an unaccompanied (and often improvised) vocal flourish just before the end of the aria, which became known as a **cadenza** because it occurs in the middle of the singer's final cadence and was sure to encourage applause.

Opera beyond Italy: Lully and Purcell

There was little enthusiasm for opera beyond Italy in the first half of the 17th century despite occasional productions of Italian opera for special occasions in Prague and (with German songs sometimes added) in the Austrian cities of Salzburg and Vienna.

The most important German composer of the early Baroque period, Heinrich Schütz, is said to have written an opera to the same libretto as Peri's *Dafne*, translated into German and performed in 1627, but no trace of the score survives.

Even in the second half of the century, the most significant composer of opera in German-speaking countries was an Italian, Antonio Cesti (1623–1669). His first two operas were written for Venice, but he later held appointments in Austria, where he wrote a dozen Italian-language operas. The best known is **Il pomo d'oro** (The Golden Apple). It was first performed in Vienna in 1668 and is in the Venetian style, with stage machinery to simulate storms, shipwrecks and collapsing towers.

The work had originally been commissioned for the wedding of Emperor Leopold I two years earlier, and was planned on a much more lavish scale than any other opera of the 17th century. There are 24 stage sets, 47 solo roles, numerous choruses and a vast orchestra in which flutes, bassoons, cornetts, trumpets and trombones were added to the normal array of strings and continuo instruments.

In France opera was at first regarded with suspicion because of its Italian origins. Despite this, Cavalli was summoned to travel from Venice to Paris in 1660 to produce an opera for the wedding of King Louis XIV. However, the French much preferred dance music and so long ballet sequences were inserted into Cavalli's opera. These were composed by the court composer, Jean-Baptiste Lully (1632–1687), ironically an Italian by birth (Giovanni Battista Lulli, before he Frenchified his name). The result was an enormously long work from which the audience came away thinking that Lully's dance music and the fascinating stage machinery were much more interesting than the unfathomable singing in Italian. Lully himself unwisely declared that opera would never work in France, as it suited neither the French language nor taste.

Nevertheless, the huge success of a French-language opera in 1671 caused Lully to change his mind, and he composed more than a dozen operas, each in five acts and described as a *tragédie en musique*. Most include prologues that glorify the king and all contain a substantial amount of dance music to satisfy the French love of ballet.

In fact, dance continued to be an important part of the French operatic tradition for the next two centuries. It is a key ingredient in the operas of Lully's most famous 18th-century successor, Rameau (some of whose works are described as *opéra-ballet*), and even 19th-century composers such as Verdi and Wagner were persuaded to add ballet sequences to their operas in order to satisfy the audiences of Paris.

Lully also established a new type of overture. Unlike the fast–slow–fast pattern of the Italian overture, the **French overture** begins with a slow and stately section featuring crisp dotted rhythms. This is followed by a fast fugal section, in which a melodic idea is chased through various sections of the orchestra. There might then be a repeat of the slow opening, or at least one dance movement, before the curtain rose.

In England there had been a tradition of presenting masques at court, particularly in the early 17th century. These staged entertainments included singing, dancing and acting, a little like the Italian *intermedio*. This tradition had come to an end by 1642 when civil war broke out, and attendance at plays and other theatrical performances was severely discouraged. By 1648, Oliver Cromwell and the puritans had control of parliament and, shortly before beheading King Charles I, they expressed their dislike of acting by ordering the destruction of theatres.

However the puritans were not averse to music, and in 1656 Cromwell gave permission to the playwright William Davenant to stage a semi-private production in London of a work described as 'recitative music'. Called **The Siege of Rhodes**, with music by five different composers, it was sung throughout (to avoid the ban on performing plays) and so has some claim to being the first English opera.

Although the music of *The Siege of Rhodes* has not survived, the diarist John Evelyn certainly thought that works of this type were operas, even if not very good ones. He describes a later Davenant production in 1659 as 'a new opera, after the Italian way, in recitative music and scenes, much inferior to the Italian composure and magnificence'.

Evelyn should certainly have known, as he had previously written enthusiastically about the operas he had attended on his travels in Italy, wryly adding his famous comment that opera 'is one of the most magnificent and expensive diversions the wit of man can invent'.

By 1659, Cromwell was dead, the puritans in disarray, and a growing belief had developed that the country was better when ruled by a monarch – albeit, one whose powers would increasingly be limited by parliament. And so the dead king's son was invited back from exile in France to reign as Charles II, the 'merry monarch'. With him came an enthusiasm for all things new and continental, particularly from the court of France's Louis XIV at Versailles, where Charles had enjoyed the music of Lully. However, Charles II had left France before opera had become established there, and England continued to enjoy masque-like works for some years to come such as John Blow's **Venus and Adonis**, 1683. One particular type, now known as **semi-opera**, was cultivated by the greatest English composer of this period, Henry Purcell (1659–1695), whose own father had sung in *The Siege of Rhodes*.

A semi-opera was essentially a spoken play interrupted by masque-like episodes containing songs, dances and spectacular stage effects. A sure indication that this was not fully opera is the fact that many of the principal characters are required to speak their words rather than sing, while the minor characters sing to entertain the principals as part of the drama.

Purcell's semi-operas include **King Arthur** (1691), which has a libretto by John Dryden about battles between the Britons of King Arthur and the Saxons, and **The Fairy Queen** (1692), which is based on an adaptation of Shakespeare's play, *A Midsummer Night's Dream*.

However, before writing either of these semi-operas, Purcell completed a work that has a claim to be the first true English opera, not simply because it was intended to be sung throughout, but because of the quality and invention of its music.

featured opera

Dido and Aeneas is a short work (about one hour in length) in three acts, and was probably intended for performance at the court of James II in 1687. However, all that is known now is that the opera was produced at a girls' school in Chelsea in 1689,

Dido and Aeneas

Dido, Queen of Carthage, cannot bring herself to admit she is in love with Aeneas, Prince of Troy. However, when Aeneas himself declares his devotion for Dido, she accepts and her court rejoices at the prospect of their union.

A sorceress, aided by witches, seeks Dido's ruin and the destruction of Carthage. They conjure up a storm to bring an end to the hunting party that the lovers are enjoying. Dido returns to the safety of her palace while the sorceress, disguised as the messenger Mercury, tells Aeneas that his destiny is to restore Troy and found Rome, and so he must leave. Aeneas laments his fate.

Aeneas's men are at the harbour and preparing to set sail. The sorceress and the witches dance at their success. Dido fears that she is being abandoned. Aeneas says he will defy the gods and stay but Dido will not endure a lover who has thought of leaving her. She insists he goes but then reveals that for Dido 'death is now a welcome guest'. In an impassioned lament she asks for those who remember her to forget her fate, at the end of which she commits suicide.

and that there were just a few later performances before the work left the stage for nearly 200 years. A libretto from the Chelsea performance survives but the earliest full score is a copy made more than 60 years after the opera was composed, and which clearly contains some omissions.

The libretto by the poet Nahum Tate was adapted from the fourth book of the *Aeneid* by the Roman poet Virgil. Tate avoided the more explicit parts of the original story and his introduction of a sorceress and cackling witches is a reminder that the influence of the masque was still alive and well at this time. The tragic ending, though, reveals that *Dido and Aeneas* was written before the age of *opera seria,* while its dance-like solos and numerous dances and short choruses suggest a keen awareness of the latest operas by Lully being produced in France:

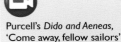

Purcell's *Dido and Aeneas,* 'Come away, fellow sailors'

Come a - way, fel-low sail - ors, come a - way, your an - chors be weigh-ing,

Purcell's music is remarkable for the way in which his recitatives faithfully reflect the tricky rhythms of the English language and flow seamlessly into the Italian style of his short arias and the French style of his dances, choruses and instrumental pieces – all from a composer who seldom left London, let alone Britain.

Purcell had a particular gift for writing ground bass arias, and of the four in this short opera, the most famous is the last. It is known as Dido's lament:

Purcell's *Dido and Aeneas*, Dido's lament

When I am laid, — am laid ⎯⎯ in earth, may my wrongs ⎯ cre - ate no trou - ble, no trou - ble in ⎯ thy breast,

At first sight, Dido's lament may seem remarkably similar to the lament composed by Cavalli more than 40 years earlier, the opening of which is shown on page 40. This type of slow, triple-time aria over a chromatically descending ground bass had become stock-in-trade for many composers in the 17th century.

Sarah Connolly as Dido and Lucy Crowe as Belinda in Wayne McGregor's production of *Dido and Aeneas* for the Royal Opera House, Covent Garden

However, closer examination reveals that Cavalli took a four-bar bass line and neatly fitted four-bar vocal phrases to it in a way that becomes predictable long before its 19 repetitions are over. Purcell, in contrast, adopts the unusual length of five bars for his ground bass, and then ensures that his vocal phrases overlap the repetitions of the bass, so that there is always a sense of the music moving forward.

The ends of Dido's phrases are marked by a bracket in the music example. Her first phrase ends on 'earth', well before the first iteration of the bass ends in bar 5. Her next phrase spans the end of the first bass pattern and the first three notes of the second, and her third phrase fits over the next four notes of the bass pattern, again finishing well short of the end of the bass line.

Later in the aria, while the same bass part repeats its ominous tread, Purcell wrings extremes of passion from the vocal line with isolated gasps of 'Remember me!' set to a single pitch and then a top G. Finally, the entire string orchestra takes over the constantly falling chromatic lines as Dido brings her life to an end.

It is tempting to speculate that Purcell might have laid the foundations of English opera had he lived beyond the age of 36. However, *Dido and Aeneas* was unique. After writing it, Purcell busied himself with semi-opera, and when *Dido and Aeneas* was revived in 1700, after Purcell's death, it was chopped into pieces in order to form masque-like interludes between the acts of an adaptation of Shakespeare's play, *Measure for Measure*.

Handel in England

In short, it seems that the English were not yet ready for entirely sung opera. Not, that is, until 1705 when three entrepreneurs realised that Italian opera, which had become such a feature of the grand tours of the day, could be transplanted to London. They hired the Theatre Royal in Drury Lane and advertised 'opera after the Italian manner: all sung'. Few of their early productions, which often included more English than Italian, are still remembered, but gradually an enthusiasm for opera developed among the public, and famous Italian singers were soon attracted to perform in London.

The craze for Italian opera heated up in 1710 when a rival opera company opened at the Haymarket Theatre. That autumn they heard that a young German composer had arrived in London. He had studied in Italy, achieved great success in Venice with his first Italian opera, and his name was George Frideric Handel (1685–1759).

Handel could compose an entire opera in a matter of weeks, sometimes aided by borrowings from earlier works, and he completed and rehearsed his first London opera, **Rinaldo**, in time to begin its initial run of 15 performances at the Haymarket on February 24, 1711. The singers were all Italian, the orchestra included sopranino and treble recorders, oboes, bassoons, four trumpets and timpani as well as strings, plus the opportunity to hear Handel's famous skill at improvising on the harpsichord, and the production included thunder and lightning, fireworks, a battle and a flock of live sparrows let loose in the auditorium during Almirena's 'Bird Song'. Copies of the libretto, with the Italian and an English translation on facing pages, allowed the audience to follow the plot, as the auditorium was not darkened as it is today.

Handel generally included several 'show-stopper' tunes in his operas. The most famous aria from *Rinaldo* (although actually borrowed by Handel from one of his earlier works) is 'Lascia ch'io pianga' (Let me weep):

The recording referenced here is sung in a concert performance by Philippe Jaroussky, a French countertenor with a particularly high range, sometimes known as 'sopranist'.

Handel's *Rinaldo*, 'Lascia ch'io pianga'

Casting of *castrato* parts is just one of the problems in presenting Handel's 40-plus operas to a modern audience. They contain some wonderful music but are governed by the many conventions of *opera seria* detailed on page 50. They were not written for the attentive audiences of today. This can easily make them seem very static without imaginative production ideas such as that illustrated opposite – a scene from Glyndebourne's 2011 production of *Rinaldo* in which the story of crusader knights is treated as a history lesson that develops into a schoolboy fantasy in a college that resembles a cross between Hogwarts and St Trinian's.

In 1719 Handel was appointed to run the new Royal Academy of Music – not the present-day college but what was hoped would become a permanent opera society for London. Handel engaged some of the best singers available and the following years saw the creation of some of his best operas, including:

■ *Giulio Cesare* (1724), an opera on an epic scale, famous for the aria 'V'adoro pupille' (I love you, eyes) sung by Cleopatra (in disguise as a servant) to Caesar with the accompaniment of two orchestras

Rinaldo at Glyndebourne

- **Tamerlano** (1724), an opera about the struggle between love and duty
- **Rodelinda** (1725), one of Handel's most popular and most typical operas.

In 1728, an enormously successful English comedy, with popular tunes arranged by Johann Pepusch, called **The Beggar's Opera** poked fun at the absurdities of Italian opera, and the next year the Royal Academy opera collapsed. Handel helped to restart the company, and achieved success with **Orlando** (1733), an opera strong on spectacle and containing a justifiably famous 'mad scene'. However, another blow followed later in 1733 when Handel's singers deserted him for a rival opera company. Handel started yet another new company at the Theatre Royal in Covent Garden, but by now it was obvious that *opera seria* in London was in decline.

Handel therefore turned to writing oratorios – sacred works for concert performance rather than for the stage. They perpetuate many of the features of *opera seria*, including recitatives and arias, but are in English and include much choral singing. Handel's oratorios include works that have never gone out of fashion with the British public since they were written, but Handel's operas were considered to be old fashioned even before he was dead. They had never been popular outside London and were quickly forgotten until rediscovered in the 20th century.

Serse (or *Xerxes*) was one of the last of Handel's operas. First produced in 1738, it was initially a total failure. In contrast, the modern revival of the work by English National Opera (shown here) proved hugely popular.

Opera Seria

The type of opera established by Scarlatti had developed into what was essentially a template for new works by 1720. This was the year in which one of the most famous of all librettists, an Italian poet writing under the pen-name Metastasio, began writing a series of *opera seria* libretti that would be set to music hundreds of times by different composers over the next century.

There was a preference for plots based on episodes from the lives of historical rulers rather than on ancient mythology. They were intended to illustrate moral values, so the comic and bawdy scenes of Venetian opera were excluded. Instead, virtue had to be rewarded, evil deeds had to be punished and a happy ending was essential, even if it contradicted historical fact.

An *opera seria* was usually divided into three acts and typically there were three groups of characters, each represented by a pair of singers:

■ Royalty, generally with the man played by a *castrato*, and the woman played by a soprano where women were allowed to perform in public (or by another *castrato* where they were not). These two roles were given to the most famous singers, who were allocated up to half of the arias in the entire production, and who were the only pair allowed to sing a duet.

- Noble confidants of the royal couple, who might be allocated three or four arias each.

- Servants, villains, abandoned lovers, false friends or other lowly characters who could expect no more than a couple of arias apiece.

After an overture, most of the opera would consist of an alternation between:

- Recitative, in which characters would interact with each other, and in which the action was taken forward.

- Aria, in which a character would express to the audience his or her feelings on the situation in which they are in, almost like a weather report.

There were often one or two duets for the principal soloists and the opera would usually finish with a joyful 'chorus', sung by all the characters who had survived until the end of the last act rather than by a separate group of singers.

The famous singers of the day insisted that they had to be alone on stage for the best arias, each of which had to occur at the end of a scene. They would finish the aria with an impressive cadenza, after which the singer would leave the stage to a huge round of applause – hence the name **exit aria** for such solos.

Composers also observed the baroque 'doctrine of affections', which dictated that music could reflect only one mood (or 'affection') during the course of a single movement, such as an aria. Even the contrasting middle section of a *da capo* aria could only offer a different perspective on that emotion, and could not introduce any greater contrast. Thus, arias usually focused on a single, simple emotion such as love, hate, joy or sorrow. In addition, principal singers expected to be presented with a range of different types of aria in order to display their vocal prowess:

- An aria about the joys of nature was often written in the style of the *siciliana* – a leisurely, lilting dance in compound time, thought to have come from Sicily.

- A character who was furious with pent-up emotion was often given a **rage aria** – fast and furious, generally in a minor key, and with sudden outbursts of angry semiquavers.

- Firm or defiant statements might be depicted in an *aria all'unisono*, in which the accompaniment is entirely in stark unison or octaves with the singer.

- An *aria di bravura* was a showcase for the singer, full of *coloratura* passages (runs, trills, wide leaps and so on).

- An *aria d'affetto* was a tender, expressive song.

- An *aria d'imitazione* might imitate the sound of bird song or hunting horns.

- An *obbligato aria* is a duet between a singer and an instrumental line played by a solo instrument such as an oboe or trumpet, or by all the violins together.

- In a *concerted aria* the singer is treated like the solo instrument in a concerto, and is supported by a particularly full orchestral accompaniment.

- A *suitcase aria* (or *baggage aria*) was a favourite song that famous singers carried in their luggage, and which they might demand be inserted into whatever opera they had been engaged to sing, whether it fitted the plot or not!

In longer arias, composers often developed the *da capo* principle into ritornello form. This would start with a substantial opening instrumental section (called the *ritornello*), after which the singer would begin, supported by a lighter accompaniment. Sections of the *ritornello*, often in different keys, would then return between the vocal passages. The fragmentary nature of these later *ritornelli* gives the form its name – *ritornello* means a 'little return' – although sometimes the complete opening *ritornello* would be repeated to end the aria.

Such a formulaic approach to opera seems strange to us today – indeed, it was mocked at the time and became the subject of considerable criticism, as explained at the start of the next chapter.

However, audiences in the Baroque era did not sit in silence and in the dark, paying close attention to the performance, as they do today. They came to the opera house to be seen by society, to play cards and talk with each other, to save the expense of heating and lighting their own homes on cold winter evenings, and some even brought along their servants to cook meals during the performance. Audiences also came to support their favourite singers, whom they would often encourage with shouts of praise at each new vocal feat. For others, the opera was little more than a casual entertainment going on in the background.

Opera seria was never favoured in France, but it remained popular in Italy, where Vivaldi claimed to have written many examples. However, relatively few of these now survive and none are regularly performed today.

The curious case of comic opera

Unlike the audiences of London, opera-goers in Venice were not entirely satisfied by the rigid conventions of *opera seria*, which effectively excluded the humour and comic characters that had formed part of 17th-century Venetian opera. And so it was that, just as opera itself had begun with the *intermedio*, a musical production between the acts of a serious play, so comic opera began with the **intermezzo** – a musical comedy played out between the acts of an *opera seria*.

The first such works had appeared in Venice by 1706, and the enthusiasm for such 'intermission pieces' soon spread to Naples, where one of the most famous examples was composed in 1733 by Giovanni Pergolesi (1710–1736). *La serva padrona* (The servant turned mistress) was written to be performed between the acts of a long-forgotten *opera seria* that he had written and is entirely typical of the *intermezzo*:

- it is only 45 minutes long

- it is in two parts (to be sandwiched between the three acts of an *opera seria*)

- it needs only two squabbling characters, a soprano and a bass, plus a silent actor

- the music is tuneful and much simpler in style than that of most *opera seria*.

The plot of *La Serva Padrona* is also typical of the *intermezzo*: it concerns a sharp-tongued maid who tricks her elderly master into marrying her, after which they both live happily ever after.

In the 1740s, the composer Baldassare Galuppi (1706–1785) teamed up with fellow Venetian Carlo Goldoni, one of Italy's best-loved playwrights, as librettist to create a long series of comic operas that were more than just intermission pieces. This type of work became known as an **opera buffa** (*buffa* is Italian for a clown or buffoon), or what might today simply be called a comic opera.

Although Galuppi's works are now largely forgotten, *opera buffa* would, in the second half of the 18th century, displace *opera seria* as the most important type of music theatre, as will be seen in the next chapter.

Nevertheless, *opera buffa* and *opera seria* are both types of number opera in which dramatic continuity was interrupted every time a singer stepped out of character to acknowledge applause at the end of an aria. Furthermore, both dramatic and musical continuity are compromised by the constant shifting between lightly accompanied recitative in which the action is advanced, and the more formal set-piece arias, which are more fully accompanied. Resolving this problem would become a preoccupation for many composers over the next century.

5. Classical Opera (1750–1815)

One of the most prominent opera composers after the death of Handel is the now almost forgotten Niccolò Piccinni (1728–1800). He showed that *opera buffa* could be a vehicle for bringing contemporary stories to the stage, and he gave the genre more substance, turning it into a true rival to *opera seria*.

The essence of comic opera at this time was the creation of a web of confusions and misunderstandings that all had to be sorted out to the audience's satisfaction before the end of the work. Piccinni and his librettists used this to develop rapidly paced finales in which a succession of musical numbers, uninterrupted by recitative, and an increasing number of characters would join in to work out the **imbroglio** (tangle) that had arisen.

Piccinni's music, which was based on the elegant simplicity of the newly emerging classical style, was central to the appeal of his comic operas, forming a marked contrast to what was increasingly felt to be the artificiality of *opera seria*.

Gluck and the reform of opera

It became increasingly obvious that *opera seria* had to change if it was to survive. The main issues being discussed at the time were neatly summarised in 1767 in the preface to the score of **Alceste**, an Italian opera by the German composer Christoph Willibald Gluck (1714–1787):

- The overture should indicate the mood of the opera that is about to start.

- Singers should not have to wait for orchestral *ritornelli* that interrupt the action.

- Composers should give singers little or no opportunity for vocal displays.

- The words should be made clear by, as far as possible, setting only one note to each syllable and avoiding long runs of notes to a single syllable.

- There should be less repetition of text within an aria.

- The second part of an aria should not be rushed through, merely in order to repeat the first part (this suggests that *da capo* aria form rarely suits the drama).

- There should be less recitative and it should be accompanied rather than *secco*; the music should move more naturally between recitative and aria.

- Melodic lines should be simpler and more flowing.

- More prominence should be given to the chorus, following the model of classical Greek drama, where the chorus commented on the action as it unfolded.

This last point confirms that the reformers wanted to go back to the classical roots from which the earliest operas sprang. Their entire approach emphasises that music should support the drama, and not be an end in itself.

Alceste also included no role for a *castrato* voice, although Gluck did write for *castrati* in some of his later operas. However, women opera singers were well established by the late 18th century and the *castrato* voice was by now in terminal decline.

Alceste was not the first of Gluck's 'reform operas'. That honour goes to his setting of the Orpheus myth (another indication that he saw reform as the process of going back to opera's earliest roots), **Orfeo ed Euridice** (1762). It is a very austere setting in comparison with Monteverdi's *L'Orfeo* – there are no wedding celebrations since Eurydice is already dead when the opera begins. Instead it opens with a mournful chorus that Orfeo punctuates with three impassioned cries of 'Eurydice'. There are only three solo parts in Gluck's setting, and the recitative is fully accompanied (making this the first opera that could be performed without continuo instruments).

Such a description may make the opera seem unattractive, but Gluck realises the aims of reform opera in some exquisitely beautiful music. Perhaps most famous of all is the aria sung by Orfeo after he has lost Eurydice for the second time – 'Che farò senza Euridice?' (What will I do without Eurydice?). The elegance and balance of its melody and the simplicity of its accompaniment are typical of the classical style (the role of Orfeo was written for a *castrato*, and is now most commonly played by a woman):

Gluck's *Orfeo ed Euridice*, 'Che farò senza Euridice'

Andante con moto

Che fa - rò   sen - za Eu - ri - di - ce,   do - ve an - drò   sen - za il mio   ben!

Mozart

The composers most closely associated with the Classical period are Haydn, Mozart, Beethoven and Schubert, who all worked in (or close to) Vienna. Beethoven wrote only one opera, which is discussed at the end of this chapter. Haydn composed a number of Italian operas for the court of his employer, but their fine music is not matched by convincing drama so modern performances are rare. However, the 2009 staging of the zany comedy *Orlando paladino* (1782) by Berlin Staatsoper suggests that it might be time to re-evaluate Haydn's stage works. Schubert, possibly the greatest songwriter who ever lived, was remarkably unsuccessful in the field of opera.

In contrast, the mature operas of Wolfgang Amadeus Mozart (1756–1791) are among the finest works ever written for the stage, and most have formed part of the standard repertory of opera houses around the world ever since they were written.

Mozart's mature operas

Opera buffa (in Italian)

Le nozze di Figaro (The Marriage of Figaro), 1786
Don Giovanni (Don Juan) 1787
Così fan tutte (Women are all like that),1790

Opera seria (in Italian)

Idomeneo, re di Creta (Idomeneus, King of Crete), 1780
La clemenza di Tito (The clemency of Titus), 1791

Singspiel (in German)

Die Entführung aus dem Serail (The abduction from the Seraglio), 1782
Die Zauberflöte (The Magic Flute), 1791

Mozart began composing operas when he was still a boy. His first *opera buffa* was written when he was 13 and performed in Salzburg. His first *opera seria* was written at the age of 14 and performed in Milan, and before either of these he had completed an opera of a type that was to become increasingly important in Germany – a ***Singspiel*** (sung play), in which spoken dialogue (in German) separates the musical numbers.

These were the three types of opera that Mozart was to develop over the rest of his short life, in the process revealing an uncanny ability to use music to characterise every facet of the personalities that populate his stage works.

Mozart and opera buffa

Mozart's three late *opere buffe* are often described as the 'da Ponte operas', after their librettist, Lorenzo da Ponte. 'Comic opera' hardly seems the right description for any of them, for Mozart uses *opera buffa* as a vehicle for the most tender, profound and dramatic musical expression in these works.

Le nozze di Figaro (The Marriage of Figaro) is a four-act opera based on a play by the French author Beaumarchais. It develops the 'servant outwits the master' idea that formed the basis of Pergolesi's *La serva padrona* into a substantial comedy about the complex relationships between a number of carefully-drawn characters:

Count Almaviva, a Spanish nobleman	The Countess, his long-suffering wife
Figaro, the Count's valet	Susanna, the Countess's maid
Bartolo, a doctor	Marcellina, an elderly housekeeper
Cherubino, a page boy (a 'trouser role')	Basilio, a music teacher
Don Curzio, a judge	Antonio, the Count's gardener

Barbarina, Antonio's daughter

Chorus of peasants, villagers and servants

A brilliant, bustling overture, reflecting the title of Beaumarchais's original play, *La Folle Journée* (The crazy day), sets the mood of the opera that follows.

Act One opens with Figaro and Susanna preparing for their wedding later that day. Susanna confides that the Count has designs on her and Figaro determines that he must outwit his master. Marcellina arrives with her old friend Dr Bartolo – Figaro once promised to marry her in return for a loan, and now she wants him to settle the debt. Cherubino rushes in to tell Susanna that he can't stop falling in love with every woman in the palace. He hides as the Count approaches. Thinking they are alone, the Count flirts with Susanna, but then he too has to hide when he hears Basilio arriving. The oily music master has come to relay

Mozart's *Marriage of Figaro*, 'Non più andrai'

the latest gossip – Cherubino has a crush on the Countess. The Count furiously leaps out of hiding, discovers Cherubino and realises in horror that the page boy overheard him flirting with Susanna. The Count orders Cherubino to leave the household and sign up as a soldier. Figaro sends Cherubino on his way, adding that this will put an end to his games with the girls:

Vivace

Non più an-drai, far-fal-lo - ne a-mo-ro - so, not-te e gior-no d'in-tor - no gi-ran-do,

Dr Bartolo, Figaro and Marcellina in *Le nozze di Figaro* at Glyndebourne Opera House

Act Two starts with the Countess lamenting that her husband no longer loves her. To shame him into changing his ways, Susanna, Figaro and the Countess hatch a plot. They will trick the Count into thinking that Susanna will meet him that night, but instead they will send Cherubino, who has not yet left, dressed as a girl. The Count is heard approaching and Cherubino hides in the Countess's closet. The Count hears noises from the closet and thinks that his wife is hiding a lover. He leaves to get tools to prise open the door, giving Susanna the chance to swap places with Cherubino, who escapes through the window. When the Count returns he is astonished to find that it is Susanna who walks out of the closet. Marcellina enters with Dr Bartolo and Basilio to ask the Count to help settle her legal claim against Figaro.

A new plan to humilate the Count is hatched in Act Three. Susanna will offer the Count a rendezvous but this time she will be replaced by the Countess in disguise. Meanwhile, Marcellina's case against Figaro collapses when it is discovered that he is her son, the result of a love affair with Dr Bartolo many years before. Later, the

Countess dictates to Susanna the request for the Count to come to the garden that night. The letter is sealed with a pin, which the Count is asked to return as a sign of agreement. The act ends with celebrations of a double marriage: Susanna and Figaro, plus Figaro's parents (Marcellina and Dr Bartolo).

Act Four takes place in the garden, late at night. Barbarina loses the pin that the Count has asked her to return. She inadvertantly reveals to Figaro (who is not in on the latest plot) that Susanna has sent a letter to the Count, and he asks Bartolo and some servants to hide in the garden and witness his wife's infidelity. Meanwhile, the Countess and Susanna swap clothes. The Countess waits for her husband, while Susanna hides. First Cherubino mistakes the Countess for Susanna and declares his love, then the Count does the same and propositions the woman he thinks is a maid but who is actually his wife. Figaro also thinks the Countess is Susanna, his new wife, and jumps out to challenge the Count – the Countess flees, followed by the Count. The real Susanna, dressed as the Countess, now comes out of hiding and eventually Figaro realises who she is. They decide to continue tormenting the Count, who comes back in time to see Figaro kissing a woman that appears to be the Countess. The Count calls for help and lights, and everyone comes out of hiding, including the real Countess. The plot is revealed, and the Count realises what a fool he has been, begs his wife's pardon for his philandering, and the opera ends with all four couples (Count and Countess, Figaro and Susanna, Bartolo and Marcellina, Cherubino and Barbarina) all rejoicing at their new-found happiness.

The Marriage of Figaro is scored for a typical orchestra of the Classical period: two flutes, two oboes, two clarinets, two bassoons, two horns, two trumpets, timpani, and strings. The recitatives are often accompanied by a fortepiano (an early type of piano), although the harpsichord, which was starting to go out of fashion by 1786, is sometimes preferred.

One of the most notable features of Mozart's writing in this opera is his depth of expression. He portrays in detail the complexity of human relationships – tenderness, trust, suspicion, grief, misunderstanding, revenge and eventually forgiveness. The lively atmosphere of an *opera buffa* is maintained, with almost every number in a major key, and with stock comedy characters such as Marcellina, Dr Bartolo and Antonio the gardener. However, the Countess's reflections on her decaying marriage echo the deep-felt emotions of the older *opera seria*.

Mozart even drew on both operatic traditions in a single aria when Dr Bartolo first arrives, keen to settle an old score with the Count. 'La vendetta' starts like a

Baroque rage aria from the age of *opera seria* ('Now for vengeance!') but in its middle section the words trip out in a stream of patter from the world of *opera buffa* ('Once I can seize on the right opportunity, I shall not let him get off with impunity').

Mozart has a wide musical vocabulary to characterise every aspect of love – the teenage crushes of Cherubino, the preying lust of the Count, the betrayed love felt by the Countess, the marital ups and downs of Susanna and Figaro, and the rekindling of an old flame by Marcellina (even though their relationship seems more like dead ashes to Dr Bartolo).

Following the principles of reform opera, Mozart preferred not to compromise the dramatic flow by using *da capo* arias with long *ritornelli*. Instead, he used structures such as **rondo form**, in which a refrain surrounds contrasting sections, creating a form that could be represented as ABACA, as in Figaro's aria 'Non più andrai' (quoted on page 58). Mozart also uses single-section songs, such as the poignant 'Porgi amor' (God of love) sung by the Countess at the start of Act Two. He designates this as a **cavatina**, which at this time meant a short, simple song with little or no repetition of text, and no use of *coloratura*.

Soon comes one of the most famous solos in the opera, 'Voi, che sapete' (Tell me what love is). This is supposedly composed by Cherubino and sung by him to a 'guitar' accompaniment mimed by Susanna but actually played by plucked strings in the orchestra. Mozart simply describes the solo as a *canzona* (a song). It is in a simple **ternary form** (ABA), with a short introduction but no intervening *ritornelli*:

Later, Cherubino enters singing the opening phrase of this tune to 'la' so the audience (and the Countess) know that it is he who is prowling around in the dark in Act Four.

Only 10 of the solo numbers in *The Marriage of Figaro* are designated as arias, compared with as many as 30 in a Baroque

Mozart's *Marriage of Figaro*, 'Voi, che sapete'

opera seria. However, vocal ensembles play a much greater role. There are six duets, three trios and a sextet. The last of these sets the scene in which Figaro is revealed to be the son of Marcellina and Dr Bartolo. Mozart casts it in a type of sonata form (a structure frequently used for the instrumental music of the day), with brilliant interplay between the six singers and the various solo lines in the orchestra.

Equally impressive is the finale to Act Two, which spans 843 bars of music. It starts with an angry duet between the Count and his wife, in which he accuses her of hiding Cherubino in her room. The music moves seamlessly into an innocent-sounding minuet when Susanna is discovered to be the person hiding in the closet. The vocal ensemble expands to become a trio as she joins in. A dramatic change of key heralds the arrival of Figaro who announces that the wedding festivities are ready to begin. However, the Count wishes to cross-examine his valet about what has been going on. The ensemble becomes a quartet as the two women try to prompt Figaro to give the correct answers to the Count. Next the gardener arrives to complain about someone jumping out of the window and breaking his flower pots, so enlarging the ensemble to a quintet. They are accompanied by increasing excitement from the orchestra – an *imbroglio* is brewing! The tempo slackens when Figaro tries to claim that he was the one who jumped out of the window, but his lie just leads to more confusion. Suddenly the initial key and mood of the finale return as Marcellina, Bartolo and Basilio burst in, demanding that the Count makes Figaro fulfil his obligation to either repay or marry Marcellina. The tempo increases twice more as the vocal ensemble expands yet again, this time to a septet who, accompanied by rushing upward scales in the orchestra, bring the finale to its hectic end.

Mozart and da Ponte immediately capitalised on the success of *Figaro* by writing a new opera to be staged the following year, 1787. Mozart catalogued it as an *opera buffa*, but it was advertised at the time as a *dramma giocoso*, a comedy that juxtaposes three distinct groups – aristocrats, servants and the middle class – each characterised with their own styles of music.

Il dissoluto punito, ossia il Don Giovanni (The rake punished, or Don Giovanni) is now known simply as **Don Giovanni.** It is a dark comedy in two acts, based on the legend of the promiscuous Don Juan, beginning with his sexual conquests and ending with the unrepentant nobleman being dragged down to hell. Highlights include the 'catalogue aria', in which Don Giovanni's servant Leporello enumerates his master's long list of seductions, and the duet 'Là ci darem la mano' (Give me your hand, my dearest, whisper a gentle 'yes'), in which the Don tries to lure a peasant girl called Zerlino from her prospective husband, brilliantly set by Mozart to the most seductive of melodies:

Mozart's *Don Giovanni*, 'Là ci darem la mano'

Là ci da-rem la ma-no, là mi di-rai di sì; ve-di, non è lon-ta-no,

Equally well known is Don Giovanni's virile 'champagne aria', in which he tells Leporello to organise a party and invite every girl he can find:

Fin ch'han dal vi - no cal-da la tes-ta, u - na gran fe-sta fa pre-pa-rar!

Don Giovanni is also famous for the use of instruments on stage during the action. In the party scene at the end of Act One, the Don's orchestra of oboes, horns and strings is first heard through an open window of his palace, as if the audience is in the garden,

Mozart's
Don Giovanni,
Champagne aria

but as the scene moves inside to the brilliantly lit ballroom, it is apparent that there are three instrumental ensembles on stage, in addition to the orchestra in the pit.

They play three simultaneous dances, each with different, but interlocking, rhythms, above which the characters continue to sing their parts. The nobility dance an aristocratic minuet, accompanied by the main onstage orchestra. The Don presses Zerlina to partner him in a country dance, accompanied by an onstage ensemble of violins and a bass (who begin with appropriate 'tuning up' noises), while Leporello distracts Zerlina's deserted fiancé by whirling him around in a galumphing 'German dance', accompanied by another onstage ensemble of violins and bass, allowing Don Giovanni to slip away with Zerlina.

An onstage orchestra also features in Act Two. Don Giovanni is eventually brought to account when a statue of the dead father of a girl he has wronged comes to life, and forces Leporello to invite him to dine with the Don as 'the stone guest'. Before the unwelcome visitor arrives, the Don's orchestra plays a selection of tunes from operas of the day, the last of which is none other than 'Non più andrai' from Mozart's very own *Marriage of Figaro*, to which Leporello responds 'that's a song I know only too well', a line that still gets a laugh today. Throughout the opera, Leporello provides the principle *opera buffa* element with witty asides of this sort, but there are few further comic episodes, for the stone guest makes a dramatic appearance to terrifying music and casts Don Giovanni into everlasting flames, as an unseen chorus 'with hollow voices' warns of the terrors that await him.

Three years after the triumphant premiere of *Don Giovanni* in Prague, Mozart and da Ponte embarked on their final collaboration, the two-act *opera buffa* **Cosi fan tutte**

Don Giovanni condemned to everlasting torment (Royal Opera House, Covent Garden)

(Women are all like that), first performed in Vienna in 1790. The plot is based on two young army officers who accept a wager that each could, in disguise, successfully woo the other's fiancée. The mysoginistic message that women can be manipulated by men was a barrier to the opera's acceptance until the 20th century. Today, a keen appreciation of the beauty of Mozart's music, along with a deeper understanding of the context of the original work and innovation in the ways in which it can be presented, has seen the work find its place in modern operatic repertoire.

Mozart and opera seria

Mozart's first major operatic success had been in *opera seria*. ***Idomeneo, re di Creta*** (Idomeneus, King of Crete) was composed in 1780 and is a three-act opera in the reform tradition of Gluck. It deals with the painful subject of a father sworn to sacrifice his son. Being *opera seria*, the king is released from his oath at the end, even though it is at the price of losing his throne.

In the last year of his life, Mozart returned to *opera seria* with **La clemenza di Tito** (The clemency of Titus), composed in 1791 based on a 1734 libretto by Metastasio.

The two-act opera was commissioned to celebrate the coronation of the Austrian Emperor Leopold II, for which the tale of the magnanimity of the Roman emperor Titus offered suitable flattery. It is among the last great masterpieces of *opera seria*.

Mozart and *Singspiel*

Works such as *The Beggar's Opera* that had led to the eventual collapse of *opera seria* in London (see page 50) were also popular in Germany, where they were translated and performed as *Singspiele* – operas in which the dialogue was spoken rather than sung to recitative. The music of a *Singspiel* was often folk-like and simple, and the plot was generally light-hearted, often including elements of magic or fantasy. A particular favourite in the middle of the 18th century were tales of European women being abducted by Turkish pirates, kept in a harem and wooed by a sultan before being rescued by their beloved. Such stories were especially enjoyed by the Viennese, who welcomed any excuse to poke fun at their former enemies, the Turks.

Mozart's **Die Entführung aus dem Serail** (The abduction from the Seraglio) was therefore not the first *Singspiel* on this subject when it appeared in 1782, but it is certainly the most famous. The three-act opera (which is also known by its Italian title of **Il Seraglio**) centres on the attempts of the hero Belmonte, assisted by his servant Pedrillo, to rescue his sweetheart Konstanze, who has been captured by pirates and imprisoned in the *seraglio* (women's quarters) of the Pasha Selim (who has a non-singing role). The rescue fails, but the Pasha magnanimously provides a happy ending.

featured opera

Mozart's last *Singpiel* was **Die Zauberflöte** (The Magic Flute). In addition to a chorus, there are 22 separate roles of which the principal six are:

Prince Tamino	Pamina (daughter of the Queen of the Night)
Papageno, friend of the prince	Papagena (who becomes Papageno's wife)
The Queen of the Night	Sarastro, the Priest of Light

The opera tells how the Javanese Prince Tamino learns wisdom in order to become worthy of Pamina and enter the temple of Isis, presided over by Sarastro, the Priest of Light. He has a magic flute to ward off evil, and he is joined on his journey by a simple but lovable bird-catcher called Papageno, who will receive his own reward in the form of Papagena, the wife of his dreams.

Opposition to this quest comes from the Queen of the Night, mother of Pamina and arch-enemy of the Priest of Light, and from Monostatos, who guards the temple and who lusts after Pamina.

The text is by Emanuel Schikaneder, who sang the part of Papageno in the first production, and who owned the popular suburban theatre in Vienna in which the two-act work was first presented in 1791. Mozart's sister-in-law sang the part of the Queen of the Night.

Schikaneder and Mozart were, like many intellectuals of their time, Freemasons. This fraternal but secret society was important in disseminating the ideals of the age of enlightenment, which regarded knowledge and tolerance as ways in which to improve society. Tamino's journey out of darkness and into light, through mysteries and rituals that parallel those in Freemasonry, is seen as an allegory of this enlightenment.

The overture begins with three chords in the key of three flats (the number three permeates the opera). As soon as the curtain rises, Tamino runs on pursued by a dragon and faints with exhaustion. The dragon is killed by three ladies who, when they notice the prince's handsome features, squabble over who should be left alone with him before all leave to fetch their mistress, the Queen of the Night.

When the prince comes round, he is greeted by Papageno who introduces himself with a jolly aria, between the sections of which he plays scales on his panpipes:

Mozart 's *Magic Flute*, 'Der Vogelsänger bin ich ja'

The three ladies return to hear Papageno pretending that he strangled the dragon, and they clap a padlock around his mouth as punishment for fibbing. Suddenly there is a clap of thunder, a mountain splits in two and the Queen of the Night appears, riding a crescent moon. She asks Prince Tamino to save her daughter whom she claims has been kidnapped by an 'evil sorcerer' named Sarastro. The men agree and the ladies remove Papageno's padlock. They give him a set of magic bells, and Tamino a magic flute, to help the pair on their way.

Papageno arrives at Sarastro's palace, where Pamina is guarded by Sarastro's servant Monostatos, who lusts after her. The bird man catches sight of the black man and each thinks the other is the devil in disguise. Papageno escapes with Pamina.

The finale to Act One begins with Tamino being led by three boys to three temples. A mysterious voice tells him to back away from the temples of Reason and Nature,

The entry of the Queen of the Night: a stage set for an 1815 production of *The Magic Flute*

but an old priest from the temple of Wisdom reveals that Sarastro is no sorcerer. He is, in fact, guarding Pamina from her mother, who is a wicked enchantress. Tamino, left alone, plays his flute and animals emerge from the woods to dance to his music. Tamino hears Papageno's panpipes and Papageno hears Tamino's magic flute, but before they meet, Pamina and Papageno are surrounded by Monostatos and his three slaves, who have been pursuing them. Papageno realises that it is time to test the magic bells and, as the pursuers hear the tinkling sounds, they become spell bound, and dance away, happily singing as they go.

Trumpets, drums and a chorus of priests and attendants announce the arrival of Sarastro, who orders that Monostatos be punished. Tamino and Pamina meet for the first time and immediately fall in love, but Sarastro orders Tamino to prove himself worthy of Pamina, and learn wisdom, by undergoing a series of ordeals.

Act Two opens with Sarastro and his priests praying to Isis and Osiris for a successful outcome to the trials. First, Tamino and Papageno are left in a darkened room and ordered not to speak to any woman. The Queen of the Night's ladies appear from nowhere to tempt them, but they remain firm.

Mozart's *Magic Flute*, Queen of the Night aria

In a moonlit garden the Queen of the Night visits her daughter and reveals that she wants to destroy Sarastro and his brotherhood of Wisdom. She gives Pamina a dagger and orders her to kill Sarastro, expressing her hatred of the Priest of Light in the rage aria to trump all rage arias, with its eye-popping *coloratura* rising high above the treble stave:

Meanwhile, the men face a second test in which they must remain silent even in the company of their future partners. Papageno chatters to an old woman who brings him water, but Tamino remains silent even when Pamina appears and begs him to speak. She is heartbroken when he doesn't say a word.

Sarastro prepares Tamino for his final trial while Papageno, bored out of his feathers, plays his magic bells and asks for a wife. The old woman re-appears, reveals herself to be the beautiful Papagena in disguise, but then instantly vanishes.

Pamina decides to kill herself using the dagger given to her by her mother. She is stopped by the three boys, who confirm that Tamino does love her, and that they will take her to him so she can help him.

Pamina joins Tamino for his final ordeal, the trials of Fire and Water. Tamino plays his magic flute to ward off evil and they pass the test unscathed. Meanwhile, Papageno thinks he will never see more of Papagena than that one fleeting glimpse. In despair he prepares to hang himself, while repeatedly delaying the moment in the hope that something will turn up. It does, in the form of the three boys, who remind him to use the magic bells. They work, and as the happy couple are reunited they can only stutter an ecstatic 'Pa-pa-pa-pa-' at the beginning of a duet in which they then go on to plan a future with many little Papagenos and Papagenas.

The happiness is darkened by the arrival of the Queen of Night who tries to attack the temple, helped by her three ladies and Monostatos. There is a sudden clap of thunder, a flash of lightning and the stage is bathed in the light of the sun: they have failed. Sarastro stands on high, Tamino and Pamina are in robes, the priests gather around, the three boys hold garlands of flowers. The Queen of the Night and her followers are vanquished by the bright light of truth and sink into the ground. Sarastro declares the victory of Tamino and Pamina over the powers of night, and, to the joy of all, he hands them the rule of his kingdom.

The Magic Flute was performed 100 times within 14 months of its completion. The reasons for its popularity are not hard to see. The production is visually spectacular, with a dragon at the start, a mountain that splits in two, three boys who travel in a flying machine (usually staged as a hot air balloon), thunder, lightning, and sudden appearances and disappearances of characters. The music is extremely varied in style, ranging from folk-like tunes designed to be sung by actors to the vestiges of *opera seria* in the Queen of the Night's rage aria and the solemn, thoughtful arias of Sarastro. The many jokes are as funny today as when they were written.

The dramatic composition of the work continues to have a universal appeal – a quest for enlightenment through knowledge, acquired on a journey during which good and evil are discoverd to be the opposite of how they are first perceived. *The Magic Flute* remains one of the most popular works in the operatic repertoire today.

Rescue opera

In the years surrounding the French Revolution of 1789 a genre known as **rescue opera** became fashionable in Paris (see page 106). Unlike the jolly abductions from Turkish harems found in *opera buffa*, the rescue opera was altogether more serious. Typically, an innocent person is imprisoned, often for their political beliefs, by a tyrant. A loyal spouse fails in an heroic attempt to rescue the prisoner, but the unexpected arrest of the tyrant ensures a happy ending.

This is basically the story of Beethoven's only opera, **Fidelio**, on which he worked for a number of years, eventually completing it as a two-act *Singspiel* in 1814, after two longer and somewhat unsuccessful versions. Beethoven, who excelled in almost every other musical genre of the age, did not seem to take naturally to opera, but the story of sacrifice, heroism and eventual triumph in *Fidelio* perfectly fitted his own political outlook. It mirrors the struggle for liberty and justice that had been at the heart of the French revolution and that was dear to Beethoven himself.

Fidelio is also the earliest *Singspiel* in the standard operatic repertory that includes **melodrama**, which in opera means orchestral music used to accompany spoken words and mime. It gives a particular sense of gothic horror to the scene in which the hero's wife, disguised as a boy called Fidelio, helps to dig what seems likely to become her own husband's grave.

6. ROMANTIC OPERA (1815–1900)

During the course of the 19th century, the popularity of opera started to increase at an unprecedented rate:

- Aristocratic court opera gave way to commercial opera, which evolved quickly in response to a growing demand from an emerging middle class audience.

- To service this demand, new opera houses were opened and older houses were enlarged, both requiring a constant supply of new works from composers.

- Technical advances, including gas and then electric lighting, and more elaborate stage machinery, made productions more exciting, adding to their popularity.

- People in countries beyond Italy, France and Germany began to establish their own national traditions of opera.

Few composers could afford to ignore opera, although some were more successful than others in writing for the stage, and a small number of composers specialised in writing opera to the exclusion of most other types of music.

Italy

Rossini

Opera was produced on an almost industrial scale in 19th-century Italy, leading to many opportunities for aspiring composers. Greatest among them in the early decades of the new century was Gioacchino Rossini (1792–1868). He was born into a musical family and by the age of 21 had written a number of successful operas including *Tancredi* (a work in the now almost defunct *opera seria* tradition) and *L'italiana in Algeri* (The Italian Girl in Algiers). The latter is a light-hearted *opera buffa* that includes some *seria* elements – a combination made famous by Rossini's hero, Mozart – and a work that is still frequently performed today.

In fact, Rossini was nicknamed 'The Italian Mozart' for his ability to write melodies that perfectly suit the voice and his skill in composing complex vocal ensembles. He also had an acute ear for orchestral colour, ensuring that the overtures to some of his now otherwise forgotten operas are still regularly heard in the concert hall.

In 1816 Rossini achieved his greatest triumph with **Il barbiere di Siviglia** (The Barber of Seville). The text is based on the first of the plays in the Figaro trilogy by Beaumarchais, Mozart's *Marriage of Figaro* being based on the second. In Rossini's *opera buffa*, which in a sense provides the 'back story' for *The Marriage of Figaro*, the young Count Almaviva, Rosina (the ward of old Dr Bartolo, who will eventually become the Countess), and Figaro, who at this stage is Bartolo's personal barber and general factotum (jack of all trades), all appear.

Rossini composed the opera at his usual breakneck speed (he claimed that the entire score took him little more than two weeks, although some parts of it were borrowed from his own earlier operas). The opening night was a near disaster. The strings on Almaviva's guitar snapped, the singer playing Dr Bartolo fell on his face at his first entrance, a cat wandered on stage and got caught in Rosina's dress, and fans of a rival composer who had set the same text some years earlier, booed and jeered at Rossini's work. But, the setback was short-lived; the quality of the piece was quickly recognised and it remains one of the most popular of all comic operas.

The overture, adapted from one Rossini had composed for an opera in 1813 and then revamped for another in 1815, has a two-part structure that had become very common by the early 19th century:

- A slow introduction (that begins with a loud chord, acting as a 'call to attention' to the audience), followed by

- A fast section containing two main ideas called 'subjects'. The first is in the main key of the piece and leads to a second, contrasting idea in a related key. Both subjects are then heard again, but with the second changed so that the music remains in the home key.

This is known as 'modified sonata form' and is a structure borrowed from instrumental music of the period, such as sonatas and symphonies. Towards the end of the second subject in this particular overture, the composer introduces one of his most famous fingerprints, now known as the **Rossini crescendo**. Ideal for adding excitement to overtures and *imbroglio* finales, it starts quietly with a repeated melody in relatively long notes played over a pulsating accompaniment. Gradually, the phrases become shorter, the repetitions more frequent, and almost imperceptibly the music begins to get louder. Gradually more instruments are added, the rhythms get faster, the notes move up to a higher register and, when the entire orchestra seems to be buzzing with excitement, Rossini unleashes the heavy brass and percussion, whipping the audience into a frenzy of excitement.

The curtain rises on the young Count Almaviva, disguised as a student, creeping around the street outside Dr Bartolo's house at dawn. He serenades Bartolo's ward, Rosina, to the accompaniment of a band of hired musicians.

Figaro enters with the most famous aria in the opera. The 'Largo al factotum' (Make way for the factotum) is a tongue-twisting showpiece for a *basso buffo* (comic bass), and it ends with the type of rapid, one-note-per-syllable style of composition known as a patter song, which was to become an essential feature of much 19th-century comic opera:

Figaro suggests to Count Almaviva that the best way to meet Rosina would be to disguise himself as a soldier and demand to be billeted at Dr Bartolo's house.

Rossini's *Barber of Seville*, 'Largo al factotum'

Bartolo, who has vain hopes of marrying Rosina himself, learns from her music teacher (Don Basilio) that he has a much younger rival in the person of Count Almaviva. Basilio suggests that he should spread slander to blacken the Count's name – advice which comes in the form of an aria containing another Rossini crescendo. An insistent pattern in the accompaniment starts quietly but gets louder and louder as Don Basilio describes how gossip will grow and grow:

The rumours, he sings, will reach such a crescendo that Almaviva's reputation will explode like cannon fire – an effect that Rossini reflects in the music. But Bartolo complains that it will all take too long to organise!

Rossini's *Barber of Seville*, Don Basilio's aria, with Rossini crescendo

The Count arrives, disguised as a drunken soldier, but the situation quickly descends into chaos. The Count threatens to attack Bartolo, neighbours are called to help and then the police are summoned, forming an *imbroglio* finale to end Act One.

Count Almaviva, Rosina and Dr Bartolo in Jonathan Miller's production of *The Barber of Seville* for English National Opera

In Act Two, the Count tries a new plan to get close to Rosina. He arrives at the house disguised as a music teacher, claiming that he is deputising for Don Basilio, who is ill. Bartolo is suspicious and asks Figaro to shave him while he keeps watch on the music lesson. Bartolo soon realises that the couple are hatching a plot.

Next comes a scene that gives an insight into how opera audiences still behaved at this time. It serves no dramatic function except to provide a minor character (Berta, a servant) with a solo. This type of song was traditionally allocated to a sub-principal and placed halfway through the last act, when vendors had a final opportunity to hawk their iced sorbets and other refreshments to the audience. The aria in this unwelcome spot became known as an ***aria di sorbetto*** (a sorbet aria or sherbet aria), and the unfortunate singer of the largely irrelevant solo had to compete with the noise of selling, followed by the sound of rattling teaspoons as hundreds of people scraped every last delicious particle from their sorbet glasses!

Bartolo sends for a lawyer to witness his marriage to Rosina before it is too late and convinces her that the person who has been pretending to court her is merely pimping on behalf of the notorious Count Almaviva. She agrees to marry Bartolo instead and admits that the Count is coming that night to elope with her. Bartolo hurries away to inform the police.

A fierce storm erupts as Figaro helps the Count into the house, giving Rossini the opportunity to write some very graphic music. The Count reveals his true identity to Rosina, who is relieved to learn that his intentions are honourable. Before they can elope, Don Basilio arrives with the lawyer who, persuaded by a pistol, agrees to witness the marriage of Rosina to the Count instead of to her guardian. Dr Bartolo arrives too late but, being relieved that he doesn't have to pay a dowry to get Rosina taken off his hands, joins in the general nuptial rejoicing.

Less than a year later, Rossini achieved another great success with **La Cenerentola** (Cinderella), an operatic version of the fairy tale in which the wicked stepmother is replaced by a stepfather, the fairy godmother by a philosopher, and Cinderella is identified by her lost bracelet rather than by her glass slipper. In addition, the work ends happily without any need for her to return to a life of drudgery.

Rossini continued to write an average of more than two operas a year until the age of 36, although after 1825 he worked mainly in Paris where his work attracted greater financial reward. **Le Comte Ory** (Count Ory), Rossini's last comic opera, received its first performance in Paris in 1828, and his final masterpiece, **Guillaume Tell** (William Tell) followed in 1829. It was Rossini's only French **grand opéra** (see page 107) and is a long and difficult work to stage.

Today *William Tell* is remembered mainly for its overture, which is among the most famous pieces of orchestral music ever written. It starts with a prelude for five solo cellos, accompanied by lower strings, which is followed by a storm, portrayed by the full orchestra. A pastoral third section features a long solo for the cor anglais, suggesting the type of melody played on alphorns by Swiss herdsmen. The overture ends with a march of Swiss soldiers, which is actually more of a rapid gallop to the finishing line than any sort of traditional march:

Rossini was 37 when he completed *William Tell*. He lived for nearly another 40 years, until the age of 76, but he never wrote another opera and he composed precious little other music in that time. Rossini had worked hard to achieve success at an early age, and he seemed content to leave his legacy at that.

The *Bel Canto* style: Bellini and Donizetti

The term **bel canto** (beautiful singing) was used in the Baroque era to describe the fine tone, sustained phrasing and vocal agility of the *castrato* voice. It was a style of singing emulated by female sopranos and tenors in Italian opera of the early 19th century, who also continued the practice of lavishly decorating their vocal line on repeats. Tenors freely used *falsetto* for top notes, and they sounded much lighter than the powerful voices that became popular in the second half of the 19th century and that are still associated with operatic tenors today.

The term *bel canto* is now often applied to the early 19th-century operatic works of Rossini, and his two immediate successors, Bellini and Donizetti.

The most famous of the 10 operas by Vincenzo Bellini (1801–1835) is **Norma** (1831). It is about a druid priestess who is betrayed by the father of her children when he falls for a younger woman. Determined to take revenge, she becomes trapped in a web of intrigue, lies and obligations, and eventually dies alongside him on a funeral pyre. Her prayer for peace in Act One, 'Casta diva' (Chaste goddess) is one of the most famous arias of the *bel canto* era.

'Casta diva' also illustrates a new style of aria that by now had replaced the *da capo* form. It begins with a slow, reflective section known as the **cavatina** (if sung at the singer's first entrance) or the **cantabile**. There is then a bridge passage (called the **tempo di mezzo**) at a moderate speed in which the action advanced, followed by a fast and increasingly exciting final section called the **cabaletta**.

This structure avoids a major disadvantage of the *da capo* aria, in which the return of its long opening section prevents the drama moving forward. In the *cavatina-cabaletta* pair the *cabaletta* is often repeated to a second stanza of text, retaining the opportunity for a singer to embellish the music, while the overall ABB form of the entire solo, with its fast B section, gives better dramatic pace than the ABA form of a *da capo* aria. Composers built pauses into the structure (just before the last vocal cadence of the *cavatina*, and usually in the *cabaletta* as well), where the orchestral accompaniment would stop in order for the soloist to deliver an unaccompanied *cadenza*.

In 'Casta diva' Norma sings the main melodic line, but the aria also includes parts for her father (a bass), the full chorus and, in the *tempo di mezzo*, a **banda** (an on-stage group of instrumentalists in costume). The aria is preceded by a fairly lengthy, orchestrally accompanied recitative for Norma, her father and the chorus, and it is rounded off by an orchestral **coda**. This all forms an uninterrupted passage of music lasting for more than a quarter of an hour known as a **scena** (scene). Like the finale, a *scena* was intended to create a natural sense of continuity in 19th-century opera, without the frequent switching between *secco* recitative and aria that interrupts the dramatic flow of a number opera.

Duets in *bel canto* opera also tended to follow the new aria structure. Recitative for both characters in conversation leads to a slow section in which the singers are first heard alone, with the same melody set to different words, before performing together. The second section, known as the **stretta**, is faster and was often repeated to allow the singers to ornament the music.

The chorus parts in *Norma* are quite extensive, but musically very straightforward, with many passages in which everyone sings in unison or in simple harmony, reflecting the fact that Italian opera houses at this time tended to use stage hands and other theatre staff to form the chorus, rather than employing professional singers.

Norma also reveals how the standard opera orchestra was continuing to grow in size. Bellini wrote the work for eight woodwind (including piccolo), four horns, two trumpets, three trombones, a cimbasso (a bass brass instrument), harp, timpani, bass drum and cymbals, and a large enough string section to balance the wind and percussion. He also required an onstage *banda* of six additional brass players.

Earlier in 1831, Bellini had scored another success with **La sonnambula** (The Sleepwalker), about a heroine who climbs into the wrong bed while sleepwalking. Other operas by Bellini still performed today include **I Capuleti e i Montecchi** (The Capulets and the Montagues), based on the same source as Shakespeare's *Romeo and Juliet*, and **I puritani** (The Puritans), a love story played out to the background of the English Civil War.

Gaetano Donizetti (1797–1848) wrote 66 operas, 29 before his first major success in 1830: **Anna Bolena**, a rather fanciful tragedy about Henry VIII's second wife, Anne Boleyn, although it stays faithful to history by ending with her execution. Donizetti had some success with stories loosely based on episodes from English Tudor history, his later tragedies including **Maria Stuarda** (Mary Stuart), 1835, about an imaginary meeting between Mary Queen of Scots and Queen Elizabeth I, and **Roberto Devereux**, 1837, about a supposed love affair between Elizabeth I and the Earl of Essex.

Donizetti's most famous tragedy is **Lucia di Lammermoor** (1835) based on the Scottish novel *The Bride of Lammermoor* by Sir Walter Scott. It is a heady mix of feuding families, wild Scottish moors, a gothic castle, a graveyard at night, hints of the supernatural, a storm, a duel, murder most bloody and the horror of a mentally deranged heroine, all of which come together to make a very model of romantic opera.

Lucia is destined for a forced marriage to revive her family's fortunes. She claims to have seen the ghost of a girl murdered by the hated Ravenswood family, but she has fallen in love with Edgar, a member of that rival clan. He has to leave for France and when he returns he discovers that his beloved Lucia has been forced to marry the wealthy Arthur Bucklaw. A storm breaks over the ruins of the Ravenswood's ancestral tower and Lucia's brother challenges Edgar to a duel. Meanwhile, the wedding guests learn the horrific news that Lucia has gone mad and murdered her new husband. She enters, stained with blood, imagining that she really married Edgar, in the famous 'mad scene'. Amid his ancestral tombs, Edgar awaits to fight a duel with her brother, only to learn that, in her madness, Lucia committed suicide. Edgar fatally stabs himself in the hope of joining her in heaven.

The 'mad scene' occurs in the last act and begins with an extended *scena* for the chorus of wedding guests and Lucia's tutor. For maximum effect, the news that Lucia has killed her husband is broken to the weddings guests while their celebrations are still in full swing. In a long and lyrical recitative the main melodic line is played by a flute (or, as Donizetti originally intended, by the eerie sound of a glass harmonica). This instrumental melody represents Lucia's deranged inner self by quoting distorted versions of music she sang earlier. After 114 bars of frequent and unsettling changes in the music, the recitative merges effortlessly into the *cantabile*, the end of which overlaps with comments from the chorus of horrified wedding guests.

The *tempo di mezzo* includes a good deal of sung dialogue for soloists and chorus, and again Donizetti smudges formal boundaries by starting a solo for Lucia at a fast tempo which almost immediately turns out not to be the *cabaletta* but another expression of her decreasing grasp on reality. It develops into an ensemble climax, after which the *cabaletta* proper begins in fast waltz time, identified by the return of the solo harmonica (or flute) – the inner voice which plays in duet with Lucia. The *cabaletta* has two verses, each ending with a response from the full company, above which Lucia rises ever higher as she imagines herself already in heaven awaiting the arrival of Edgar.

Like Rossini, Donizetti was also an accomplished writer of comic opera. All three of his works outlined below continue to attract full houses for opera companies around the world.

L'elisir d'amore (The Elixir of Love), 1832, tells the story of a shy village lad who is in love with the beautiful Adina. She doesn't return his feelings and instead gives her heart to a dashing army sergeant the moment she first claps eyes

Donizetti's *L'elisir d'amore*, Obbligato duet

Jonathan Miller's production of *The Elixir of Love* at English National Opera updates the setting from a 19th-century village in the Basque country to an American diner in the 1950s

on him. A quack doctor arrives, describing his enormous range of potions and pills in the obligatory patter song. He sells the unhappy boy a 'love potion' that seems to give him the necessary courage, probably because it is simply a bottle of wine. After various mishaps and uncertainties, true love conquers all. The doctor is amazed that his 'elixir' seems to have worked, and the sergeant resigns himself to having to find new conquests

La fille du régiment (The Daughter of the Regiment) was written in 1840 when Donizetti was living in Paris. It has a French libretto, with spoken dialogue between the musical numbers, making it *opéra comique* (see page 106) rather than *opera buffa*.

Donizetti's *La fille du régiment*, Tonio's aria

Marie is a tom-boy who has been raised by an entire regiment of doting troops. They are defending a Swiss village when Marie is saved from falling down an alp by a handsome mountaineer called Tonio. The young pair have fallen in love but it is understood that she must marry a soldier, so Tonio enlists in the regiment, greeting his new friends with one of the most demanding arias ever written for a tenor as it culminates in a succession of top Cs, of which these are only the first two:

Pour mon â - - me Quel ___ des - tin ___

The love of Marie and Tonio is thwarted by the Marquise of Birkenfeld, who claims to be Marie's aunt and whisks her off for lessons in becoming more feminine – in preparation, it seems, for marriage to the gawkish son of the monstrous Duchess of Krakenthorp (a non-singing comedy role). The regiment arrives to rescue Marie but when the Marquise reveals that Marie is actually her daughter, born out of wedlock, Marie declares that she cannot go against her own mother's wishes in the question of marriage. However, the Marquise is so moved by Marie's attachment to the regiment that raised her that she blesses the union of Marie and Tonio, resulting in a finale of general rejoicing.

Dawn French in the non-singing role of the Duchess of Krakenthorp and Ann Murray as the Marquise of Birkenfeld in *La Fille du Régiment* at the Royal Opera House, Covent Garden

Donizetti's final comedy, **Don Pasquale**, is an *opera buffa* in Italian, although it was first performed in Paris in January 1843. Following a model that had recently become popular in France, Donizetti gave the opera a **pot-pourri overture** – that is, an overture consisting of a selection of tunes from the opera itself.

The elderly bachelor Don Pasquale is furious that his nephew Ernesto wants to marry a poor girl named Norina, whom Pasquale has never seen, instead of the rich bride that has been found for him. Pasquale decides that he himself must marry a young wife to whom he can leave all his wealth, thus disinheriting Ernesto.

Pasquale's friend, Dr Malatesta, comes up with a plan to teach the old fool to act his age. The beautiful Norina pretends to be Malatesta's sister and hopeful for the hand of Don Pasquale in marriage. The elderly bachelor nearly has a heart attack when he sees how young and beautiful she is, but recovers in time to sign a fake wedding contract. Instantly, the new 'wife' changes. She won't allow Pasquale to kiss her, but she embarks on a spending spree to end all spending sprees. She doubles the servants' wages, and the house fills up with new dresses, hats, shoes and furniture while Pasquale receives the incoming bills with increasing horror.

Eventually Norina deliberately drops a letter indicating that she plans to meet a secret lover in the garden that night. Don Pasquale persuades Dr Malatesta to come and witness a showdown. The next example is from the *stretta* (the final fast section) of the duet in which they plot what will

Donizetti's *Don Pasquale*, Don Pasquale and Dr Malatesta duet

happen. It is another example of Donizetti's fondness for lively dance-like tunes, and the subsequent patter sections even include patter song in duet:

That night in the garden Pasquale catches his 'wife' kissing a stranger (he doesn't recognise that it is Ernesto) and he orders her to leave. However, he is puzzled when she refuses to go unless he allows Ernesto to marry Norina. At last they reveal to Don Pasquale how he has been bamboozled and that he was never really married to Norina – who is, in fact, the girl Ernesto had been hoping to marry from the start. Realising what a fool he has been, Don Pasquale gives the young couple his blessing, along with half of his worldly goods, and all ends happily as it should.

Verdi

Less than a year before the first performance of *Don Pasquale*, an as yet little known Italian composer called Guiseppe Verdi (1813–1901) scored his first great success with the opera **Nabucco** (1842). It tells the biblical story of the Jews held captive in Babylon by King Nebuchadnezzar (Nabucco). The highlight of the work is the Chorus of Hebrew Slaves, sung by the entire chorus in hushed unison before bursting into glorious and *fortissimo* four-part harmony:

Largo
tutti sotto voce

Va, pen - sie - ro,   sull'a - li do - ra - te;   Va, ti   po - sa sui cli - vi, sui col - li,

Verdi's *Nabucco*,
'Va Pensiero'

Rossini spoke highly of 'Va, pensiero', describing it as a grand aria for choir, and Donizetti prepared the first performance of the entire opera in Vienna. Even more important than the approval of the two previous generations of Italian opera composers was the approval of the public. A political movement known as *Il risorgimento* (the resurgence) was pressing for Italy to become a single nation state, rather than a collection of small territories, some of which were governed by other countries. Verdi's 'Va, pensiero', with its text about a lost homeland and its sing-along melody, became an anthem of the movement and it is still an unofficial national anthem of Italy to this day.

Furthermore, the movement was keen to see the popular Vittorio Emmanuele II, King of Sardinia, installed as the figurehead of a united Italy. Verdi found himself becoming increasingly linked with this ambition and eventually the movement adopted the slogan *Viva Verdi* (Long live Verdi) as code for *Viva V.E.R.D.I. – Viva Vittorio Emmanuele, Re D'Italia* (Long live Victor Emmanuel, King of Italy). Even though there is probably some historical gloss on this legend, Verdi was elected to the parliament of the new Kingdom of Italy in 1861 and was later named as a Senator by the King. When Verdi died in 1901 he was given a state funeral and the people lined the street to sing 'Va, pensiero' as his coffin passed by.

By the age of 37 Verdi had completed 16 operas, but none matched the early success of *Nabucco*. There are occasional performances today of **Louisa Miller** (1849), and **Macbeth** (1847) is sometimes staged, although almost always in Verdi's 1865 revision of the work. Verdi was working as a staff composer, having to write at a furious pace to the specific demands of opera houses and singers. He later referred to these as his 'galley years' – a reference to slaves chained to their oars in Roman galleys.

During this period of training, Verdi learnt many of the principles that would stand him in good stead for the rest of his operatic career. One was the need to avoid rigid distinctions between comic and tragic works. Another is that drama needs to be relevant to a contemporary audience and can be at its most powerful when juxtaposed with comedy. Verdi had a keen sense of the relationship between drama and music, and he realised that he could not achieve his aims by just accepting a finished libretto and setting it to music. He needed to manage the entire creative process, selecting the subjects for his operas and giving librettists precise directions on what to write where necessary.

Verdi's mature works reflect the changes that were occurring in opera in the middle of the 19th century. These included dropping conventions such as entrance arias and ensemble finales if they didn't suit the dramatic situation, creating a more innovative role for the chorus, and writing for the modern operatic tenor voice, which needed power rather than flexibility at the top of the range as larger opera houses became fashionable.

Verdi's mature operas

Rigoletto, 1851
Il trovatore, 1853
La traviata, 1853
Les vêpres siciliennes, 1855
Simon Boccanegra, 1857/1881
Un ballo in maschera, 1859
La forza del destino, 1862
Don Carlos, 1867
Aida, 1871
Otello, 1887
Falstaff, 1893

Verdi developed a more conversational type of duet in which characters exchange ideas as in spoken dialogue, rather than singing long solos. He also often made use of *arioso* – a vocal style more speech-like than aria, but more melodic than recitative, in which the orchestra carried the main melodic line (often a repeating motif), against which the singers could unfold a narrative in a relatively natural manner.

In many of his later works, Verdi used a short musical idea, often described as a **motto theme**, which returns at certain key points in the opera to represent something of dramatic significance. These themes are not used like Wagner's tightly integrated *leitmotifs* (see page 126) but they do often serve to remind the audience of the significance of past events. For example, in *Otello* the music of Otello's passionate love duet with his wife Desdemona is heard again three acts later when he kisses her before strangling her for supposed infidelity. It returns in the final bars of the opera when Otello, after realising that he has unjustly killed Desdemona, stabs himself and kisses his lifeless wife for the final time before joining her in death.

featured opera

Verdi was commissioned to write a new opera for the 1851 carnival season in Venice and he asked his librettist, Francesco Piave, to prepare a text based on *Le Roi s'amuse* (The king amuses himself), a French play by Victor Hugo. The opera was eventually named after its principal character, **Rigoletto**.

Verdi and Piave both knew that the subject was a risky undertaking as the work paints a picture of a promiscuous king with no sense of morality, who treats women as his playthings and who seduces his own jester's daughter. Hugo's play had been banned in Paris after just one performance and theatre censorship in Italy was becoming increasingly repressive at this time.

After much worry and negotiation, Verdi and Piave were permitted to stage *Rigoletto* providing the central character was downgraded from a French king to a 16th-century Italian duke of a region that no longer had any political importance. Astonishingly, the real essence of the plot could remain unchanged, allowing Verdi to realise his ambition of creating a tragicomedy about a jester ruined by his own jealousy. The work also retains its underlying theme of corruption in high places, which resonates with audiences today as potently as it did in Verdi's own time when frustration with the governments of some of Italy's many small states was reaching boiling point in the *risorgimento* movement.

The principal characters in the opera are:

The Duke of Mantua	Rigoletto, the Duke's jester
Count Monterone, the Duke's enemy	Gilda, Rigoletto's daughter
Count Ceprano	Giovanna, Gilda's chaperone
Sparafucile, a hired assassin	Maddalena, Sparafucile's sister

Chorus of courtiers, etc (male voices only)

The first half of Act One could almost be from a comic opera. The curtain rises on a splendid ballroom in the Duke of Mantua's palace, where a party is in full swing. An onstage *banda* accompanies a sequence of dance numbers, above which we learn that the Duke is on the prowl for new female conquests. The dancing is interrupted for his first aria in which the Duke declares every woman to be fair game. Verdi deftly paints his character in music that has immense surface charm, but no depth.

The mood changes with the arrival of Rigoletto, whose wit relies on a vicious tongue. His loathing for the sycophantic courtiers, and their gambling and drinking, is matched only by the hatred of courtiers for Rigoletto. They think that that the hunch-backed jester is hiding a secret lover, while Rigoletto suggests to the Duke that the young Countess Ceprano would be an easy conquest if her husband could be done away with.

Suddenly Count Monterone forces his way into the party. His daughter has been seduced by the Duke. Rigoletto intervenes to mock Monterone's concern for his daughter's 'precious honour' but, before the jester realises that he has gone too far, the distraught father turns and publicly curses the Duke and his jester.

After Monterone has been thrown out, the scene changes to a quiet backstreet where Rigoletto lives, next to the palace of Count Ceprano. It is late at night and the jester ruminates on what has just happened in a short but dramatic monotone that forms the motto theme of the work:

This is the motto with which the opera began, heard in the opening bars of its short prelude, and it occurs whenever Rigoletto recalls the curse, including at the very end of the opera when the curse is most horrifically fulfilled.

Rigoletto is intercepted by Sparafucile, a professional assassin. Set to the most exquisite melody for muted solo cello and bass, with an almost playful pizzicato accompaniment, Sparafucile delivers a spine-tingling message in *arioso* that he will see off anyone's rival for a price. Rigoletto replies that he does not yet have need of such a service. He reflects on his unhappy life at court and the evil omen of the curse motto is heard once more before he hurries indoors.

Once inside, it is discovered that the woman he keeps locked away is his daughter, Gilda. Rigoletto's wife is dead and she is all he has left. He is so terrified that she might be raped that he will only let her leave the house to go to mass. Rigoletto hears a noise and goes outside to investigate. Behind his back, the man he fears most – the Duke – slips into Rigoletto's house, disguised as a student. There the Duke discovers that the girl he picked up after church is none other than his own jester's daughter. The Duke declares his passionate love to Gilda, without revealing his true identity, but flees when he hears noises in the street. They come from his own courtiers, who are intending to abduct the girl they think must be Rigoletto's mistress. When the men bump into the jester in the street, they tell him they are after Ceprano's wife. They blindfold Rigoletto and get to him hold their ladder:

It is only after all has gone quiet, apart from Gilda's cries in the distance, that Rigoletto rips off the blindfold. As he realises that he has just assisted in the abduction of his own daughter, Rigoletto remembers Monterone's curse.

Verdi's *Rigoletto*, 'Zitti, zitti'

Act Two opens with the Duke lamenting the loss of his Gilda when some of his courtiers burst in to tell him that they have Rigoletto's 'mistress' locked in an upstairs room. The Duke immediately realises that it must be Gilda, and his sadness turns to lust as he goes to find her.

As soon as the Duke has left, Rigoletto appears. At first he puts on a brave face, but once he realises what the Duke is doing, he breaks down, admits to the courtiers that the girl is his daughter, and pleads to be allowed to see her. Gilda enters in tears and explains in private to her father how she has been shamed by the man she thought loved her. Rigoletto tells her he has one thing to do, and then they must leave the city. As Count Monterone is dragged through the palace on the way to his death, Rigoletto promises that the old man will be avenged as he plots a terrible vendetta against the Duke:

'Si, vendetta' shows how successfully Verdi could adapt traditional forms to specific dramatic purposes. It is a duet, but while Rigoletto is bent on vengeance, his daughter is begging him to let the Duke live because she still loves him. They are therefore

Video 28

Verdi's *Rigoletto*, 'Si, vendetta'

heard separately for much of the duet. Rigoletto sings entirely alone in the first verse, but during Gilda's verse he adds interjections of 'vengeance' and 'no', just as she begs Rigoletto to exercise forgiveness during his second solo. Although they finally sing together, each maintains their distinctive stance and separate words until the end.

Act Three takes place at a dilapidated inn on a lonely riverside at night. Rigoletto has availed himself of Sparafucile's offer. The assassin's sister, Maddalena, is the bait that has lured the Duke into a trap. Rigoletto has brought his daughter to witness the true nature of the man she still loves.

This final act requires a split set in which the audience can see what goes on inside the inn between Sparafucile, Maddalena and the Duke, as well as being able to see the outside, where Rigoletto and his daughter are looking on. Gilda does not have to wait long to discover the Duke's true nature. He reveals that he believes a woman to be as flighty as a feather in the wind, in the most famous aria in the opera:

Allegretto

La don-na è mo-bi-le   qual piu-ma al ven - to,   mu - ta d'ac - cen - to

Verdi's *Rigoletto*, 'La donna è mobile'

Verdi knew that 'La donna è mobile' would be a show-stopper (as it still is) and he went to some lengths to ensure that the song wasn't leaked or even overheard before the first performance. Some described it as brash, but that was Verdi's intention – to portray the unrelenting shallowness of the Duke that the love-struck Gilda ignores.

Sparafucile signals for his sister to come downstairs. Maddalena enters, provocatively dressed, and immediately start flirting with the Duke, while Gilda looks on horrified from outside. Verdi then begins his most famous of all ensembles, the vocal quartet 'Bella figlia dell'amore' (Sweet daughter of love). Inside the inn, the philandering Duke promises to be a faithful lover while Maddalena teases him that he is the lying kind of lover. Outside the inn, the heartbroken Gilda blames herself for not realising that the Duke is the lying kind of lover, while her father declares that the Duke is just a liar, and no kind of lover at all. The quartet is, in effect, a double duet with four very distinctive melodic lines heard simultaneously in counterpoint.

Rigoletto does not want his daughter to witness what is about to happen, so he tells her to disguise herself in male clothing and meet him later. Rigoletto then meets Sparafucile to pay a deposit for the assassination.

A storm starts to gather, for which Verdi specifies a bass drum behind the scenes (in addition to the one in the orchestra), a thunder machine and, most innovative of all, parts for the male voice chorus to hum chromatically in the wings, conjuring up the sound of a howling wind.

The Duke is invited to stay the night and, while waiting for Maddalena to join him, falls asleep while singing a fragment of 'La donna è mobile'. As the storm rages Gilda unexpectedly returns, wearing male clothing, and overhears Maddalena begging her brother not to assassinate the Duke. Sparafucile agrees that if anyone comes to the inn before midnight, he will kill that person instead. On hearing this, Gilda resolves to die for her faithless lover. She bangs on the door, Sparafucile knifes her, and her body is stuffed into a sack.

As midnight approaches, the storm eases and Rigoletto returns for his moment of vengeance. He pays Sparafucile the balance that is due and drags the sack containing the body of what he believes to be the Duke to the water's edge.

La donna è mobile in Jonathan Miller's production of *Rigoletto* for English National Opera

Suddenly Rigoletto hears 'La donna è mobile' being sung in the distance. It is the Duke and so he must still be alive! Rigoletto frantically cuts open the sack and, instead of the body of the Duke, finds his own daughter who has been fatally wounded. She begs her father to forgive her before dying in his arms. As the motto theme is heard for the last time Rigoletto realises that the curse has wreaked its revenge on him. He collapses in grief beside his dead daughter as the curtain falls on the final act.

Audiences have always loved *Rigoletto*, but some critics were sceptical at first, being troubled by the opera's realistic portrayal of the less appealing sides of human life and puzzled by its novelty. At the end of Gilda's main aria, the courtiers who are arriving to abduct her unconventionally start singing before she has finished, thus tightening the dramatic pace. Then where is the customary full-cast finale to complete the work? The opera ends with only two people on stage, and one of those is dead. And why does the principal character, Rigoletto, have no conventional solo aria?

However, everyone loved the wealth of melody in *Rigoletto*, as well as the care with which Verdi used music to paint his characters. For instance, Gilda's journey from innocence to heartbreak is depicted in melodies that develop from the joyous, bubbly figures that she sings in Act One, through a sombre realisation of the situation in which she finds herself in Act Two, to sighs of despair and broken scraps of melody in Act Three. The music for the Duke, in contrast, is as deliberately superficial in the last act as it was in the first. His is not a character that develops during the opera.

Although *Rigoletto* is usually staged as its original censors required (in 16th-century Mantua), one of the most successful updates to any opera has been Jonathan Miller's 1982 production of *Rigoletto* for English National Opera, which went on to be re-staged for decades. A scene from Act Three is shown opposite.

Taking the opera's themes of vendetta and systemic violence as his cue, Miller set the opera in the criminal underworld of Little Italy in 1950s' New York, where the Duke is a mafia boss who orders the killing of Monterone, the head of a rival family. The work opens in a swanky hotel where the Duke is holding a cocktail party for his mobsters and their molls, and where Rigoletto is the Duke's sidekick and dogsbody. Gilda and Rigoletto live in an anonymous New York tenement, next to Ceprano's nightclub, while Sparafucile and Maddalena run a lonely dockside bar. The bar even includes a jukebox (or, as Miller points out, a 'Duke box') in which the Duke inserts a coin to give the impression that it plays the accompaniment to his performance of 'La Donna è mobile'.

Verdi followed up the success of *Rigoletto* with **Il trovatore** (The Troubadour, 1853), a complex story which culminates in the Count di Luna unwittingly putting to death the brother he had spent his life searching for. 1853 also saw the premiere in Venice of **La traviata** (The Fallen Woman). The libretto by Piave is based on *La dame aux Camélias* (The Lady of the Camellias), a play adapted from a novel of the same name by the Frenchman, Alexandre Dumas *fils*, published in 1848. It tells the story of a young woman despised by society who gives up everything for true love, only to be misunderstood and eventually to die of tuberculosis in the arms of her lover.

Verdi's trilogy of middle-period operas (*Rigoletto*, *Il trovatore* and *La traviata*) at once gave the composer a permanent place in the repetoire of every professional opera company. He had discovered that successful opera in the second half of the 19th century meant choosing strong subjects that explore the full range of human experience. His later works are equally fine, but some had to wait until the 20th century before being widely appreciated.

Les vêpres siciliennes (The Sicilian Vespers) was written as a French grand opera (see page 107) for Paris, where it was not a great success. The plot is based on a real and bloody event in Italian history, making the work too politically sensitive to stage without alteration during the struggles of the *risorgimento*. It was not until after the unification of Italy in 1861, that the Italian version normally heard today appeared.

This has the title *I vespri siciliani* and does not include the long ballet sequence that Verdi had included to satisfy the French taste for dance.

Simon Boccanegra was another collaboration with Piave, who based his libretto on a play about a 14th-century ruler of Genoa. In 1881 Verdi revised the original 1857 version, and it is this later version that is most commonly heard today.

Un ballo in maschera (A Masked Ball, 1859) is a rather fanciful account of a real historical event, the assassination of King Gustav III of Sweden in 1792. The political nature of the plot saw Verdi embroiled in legal battles and more difficulties with censorship.

La forza del destino (The Force of Destiny, 1862) was a commission from Russia, where it was first performed. The libretto (by Piave) is based on a Spanish drama that tells the story of two young lovers separated by circumstances beyond their control. He becomes a monk, she a hermit. They are only reunited in death brought about by unrelenting family honour. The cruel fate of destiny portrayed in the original version was toned down a little in Verdi's 1869 revision, in which the man no longer flings himself off a cliff, but is persuaded to trust in heaven, where his beloved awaits.

Don Carlos (1867) was composed for Paris, and is another grand opera in five acts written to a French libretto. It is based on the life of the 16th-century Carlos, Prince of Asturias in Spain, whose fiancée (Élisabeth de Valois) was married off to his own father as part of a peace treaty. The work is opera on a really grand scale, with huge processions and imposing crowd scenes, and it is also very long when the ballet demanded by the French is included. Verdi later sanctioned various cuts as well as a version in Italian (*Don Carlo*) in which language the work is usually heard today.

After *Don Carlos*, Verdi retired to the farm that he had purchased nearly 20 years earlier. When Isma'il Pasha, the ruler of Egypt, approached him for an opera on an Egyptian subject to stage in Cairo, Verdi tried to discourage him by requesting a vast payment which, it turned out, Pasha was willing to offer.

The result was **Aida** (1871), a grand opera in four acts, set in the time of the Pharaohs. It has an Italian libretto that was based on a scenario devised by a French Egyptologist and on ideas from *Nitteti*, an old Metastasio libretto dating from 1756. The work was not, as was once thought, written for the opening of the Cairo Opera House or the Suez Canal, but it was part of the ongoing festivities to celebrate the 'westernisation' of Egypt under Pasha's rule.

Aida, the daughter of the King of Ethiopia, has been captured by the Egyptians. She serves as a slave to the Pharaoh's daughter, Amneris, and has not revealed her royal status. Both Aida and Amneris love Radames, captain of the Egyptian army. Radames

Aida at English National Opera

captures Aida's father in battle, without realising that he is the king, returning in triumph in a famous 'Grand March'. The Pharaoh pardons all those captured in the battle and offers Amneris to Radames in marriage as reward for the victory.

Aida's father persuades her to trick Radames into betraying his country. The plan is overheard by Amneris and Radames is sentenced to be buried alive for treason. When he is sealed into a tomb he discovers Aida is there, preparing to die with him. In a poignant split-set, the young lovers in their tomb rapturously sing as their spirits soar to heaven, while in the temple above Amneris prays for the soul of her lost love.

Aida was not to be Verdi's last opera. His publisher, aware of the huge popularity of Verdi's music, persuaded him to write another, which was to turn out to be one of the composer's greatest achievements.

Otello was first staged in Milan in 1887, when Verdi was 73. The librettist, Arrigo Boito (who was also a composer in his own right), skilfully condensed Shakespeare's tragedy *Othello* for the operatic stage, focusing on the evil of Iago and the role of evil in the world. Many commentators regard this intense work as Verdi's greatest opera, but the composer was to be inspired again by his love of Shakespeare.

The premiere of ***Falstaff*** took place in 1893, when Verdi was almost 80 years old. It was his last opera, his only successful comedy, and the composer claimed that he wrote it purely for his own pleasure. The libretto by Boito creates an affectionate portrait of the larger-than-life Sir John Falstaff, Shakespeare's preposterously vain and boastful knight, drawing on material from *The Merry Wives of Windsor* as well as *Henry IV* Parts 1 and 2. More than any previous Verdi opera, the music sweeps along in a continuous flow, with little sense of stopping for set-piece arias. The orchestration is brilliant and Verdi proves to be as inventive as ever, particularly when he ends the work with a mock-serious fugue in which the entire company sends the audience home chuckling with the message that those who laugh last laugh best.

Verdi so dominated Italian opera in the second half of the 19th century that few of his contemporaries seem to have been able to produce works that achieved lasting success beyond the shores of Italy. One exception is **La Gioconda** (The Happy Girl) by Amilcare Ponchielli (1834–1886). With a libretto by Boito, it was first staged in Milan in 1876 and is grand opera on a lavish scale. The work is set against the backdrop of 17th-century Venice during carnival, and includes spectacular crowd scenes and a pirate vessel that bursts into flames at the end of Act Two.

Being a grand opera there is, of course, the obligatory ballet sequence, which has become famous in its own right, particularly after it was used in Walt Disney's classic film animation, *Fantasia* (1940). The Dance of the Hours, supplied with words, even became a novelty pop hit in the 1960s:

Ponchielli's *La Gioconda*, The Dance of the Hours

Verismo and Puccini

Before 1890 operas had seldom been about everyday life. Unless the work is a comedy, the characters in opera have mostly been historic or aristocratic – or both. However, in 1890 Pietro Mascagni (1863–1945) won a competition for young Italian composers who had not yet had an opera performed on stage. Mascagni's prize was to have his opera **Cavalleria rusticana** (Rustic Chivalry) performed in Rome, and it created a sensation.

The libretto is based on a short story by Giovanni Verga, an Italian author famous for a new literary style called **verismo** (realism), in which he paints a frank picture of peasant life on his native island of Sicily, including its more sordid and violent aspects.

The term *verismo* was soon applied to a new trend in Italian opera during the period from 1890 to about 1920. *Verismo* operas feature extremes, with passionate, late-Romantic melody contrasting with scenes of brutality, violence and terror. Characters are often motivated by jealousy, and the need for revenge usually results in at least one good stabbing – and preferably multiple deaths – during the course of the opera. Critics of *verismo* opera, and there have been many, often describe it as sensationalist. However, the cultural importance of the genre is seen in its great popularity with the public and hence with the managers of opera houses.

Cavalleria rusticana takes place on Easter Sunday in a small Sicilian village. The orchestral prelude is interrupted, before the curtain rises, by the sound of Turiddu serenading Lola, who is now another man's wife. When he returned from military service he had discovered that Lola, who had been his fiancée, had dumped him and had married a villager named Alfio. Out of spite, Turiddu had then seduced Santuzza, an orphan, leaving her pregnant. Lola, overcome with jealousy, decides to win back Turiddu despite the fact that she is now married to Alfio.

As the grand centrepiece of the opera begins, a choir and organ are heard offstage, as if from the inside of the village church. The villagers and clergy, formed from the main chorus, then process into the church singing a magnificent Easter Hymn with full orchestral accompaniment. Between its phrases the offstage choir can be heard singing alleluia. Santuzza's voice carries above the entire ensemble, but she has to remain outside the church for she has lost her honour and cannot attend mass.

Santuzza confronts Turiddu about his promise to marry her, but when he throws her to the ground and follows Lola into church, Santuzza hurls an Easter curse at him. Burning with jealousy, she tells Alfio that his wife has been unfaithful. He threatens vengeance on Turiddu and Santuzza immediately regrets what she has started.

A famous orchestral **intermezzo** precedes the second half of the drama:

Andante sostenuto

While Turiddu is leading the villagers in a drinking song outside his mother's wineshop, Alfio arrives, overcome with rage. He refuses a drink, which Turiddu then pours on the ground. Alfio challenges Turiddu to a duel with knives which Turiddu accepts

Mascagni's *Cavalleria Rusticana*, orchestral intermezzo

in the customary Sicilian manner by biting his opponent's ear until it bleeds. Turiddu nervously asks his mother to look after Santuzza if he should not return, and then leaves for the duel. The square fills with villagers, anxious to know what is happening. A woman runs in screaming that Turiddu has been butchered. Santuzza shrieks wildly and collapses. Turiddu's mother faints and the crowd looks on in horror at the events of that Easter Sunday in Sicily.

The success of Mascagni's opera was matched two years later by **Pagliacci** (Clowns) by Ruggero Leoncavallo (1857–1919), who wrote his own libretto.

In the middle of a lively prologue, Tonio the clown steps in front of the curtain to declare that the story which follows is true, and that clowns have feelings, just like everyone else.

It is the feast of the Assumption in a village in the far south of Italy, and a troupe of clowns is announcing that evening's performance. Canio, head of the troupe, is furious that his wife Nedda is paying too much attention to Tonio, and he warns the local men not to flirt with her. Some of the villagers go to vespers while others resort to the tavern. Tonio finds Nedda alone but she strikes him when he tries to kiss her.

Tonio then discovers that she has a lover, Silvio, in the village and they are planning to run away together after that evening's performance. He tells Canio, who demands to know who Nedda is seeing. She refuses to say, even when threatened with a knife, and Tonio advises him to wait until later when all will become clear. In the opera's most famous aria, 'Vesti la giubba' (Put on the costume), Canio dons his costume and make-up, realising that he has become the jealous husband that he must play in that night's performance, even though his heart is breaking.

After an orchestral intermezzo, Tonio blows a trumpet and another clown bangs a drum to encourage the crowds to come to see their play. As it unfolds, distinguished by Leoncavallo's archaic minuets and gavottes, it becomes apparent that the play is mirroring the 'real-life' scenario of the first part of the opera. Nedda and her onstage lover plot to poison Pagliaccio (played by her husband, Canio). When Taddeo, playing the role of a servant, assures Pagliaccio of his wife's innocence, Canio finally snaps and, falling out of character, demands that Nedda reveal the name of her lover.

She tries to continue playing her part, and the audience of villagers applaud the seeming *verismo* of the acting. Canio shouts that he is no longer a clown and the crowd suddenly realises that they are no longer watching a play, but real life. Canio fatally stabs his wife and, as her lover Silvio rushes forward to help, Canio murders him, too, before announcing, in speaking tone, 'The comedy is over'.

Pagliacci was as great a success as *Cavalleria rusticana* despite (or perhaps because of) the many similarities between the two works. Both are set in small Italian villages on religious holidays, in both cases a spurned lover becomes an informer on an unfaithful wife, triggering the cuckolded husbands' crimes of passion, both include solo singing within their orchestral prologues, both are short works that include an intermezzo at their midway point, and both end with a single line of spoken dialogue.

They also share the similarity that, while both composers went on to write many other operas, none achieved the success of these first operatic ventures (Leoncavallo's *La bohème* is occasionally staged, but it has long been eclipsed by the more famous setting by Puccini – see page 95).

Cavalleria rusticana and *Pagliacci* seem destined to be joined at the hip for ever more, since each is too short to stage on its own, but billed together (as they always are) 'Cav and Pag' make a full evening's programme.

Another composer of the period who is now mainly remembered for one opera is Umberto Giordano (1867–1948). **Andrea Chénier** (1896) is loosely based on the real story of the French revolutionary poet who was guillotined for alleged crimes against the state. Giordano's version adds spying and intrigue, as well as love interest in the form of a French aristocrat who dies with the poet at the end of the opera.

Andrea Chénier has remained popular in part because of its fine arias for soprano and tenor, which are often heard in recitals and operatic selections. The same is true of **Adriana Lecouvreur** (1902) by Francesco Cilea (1866–1950). The opera is another combination of fact and fiction, this time based on the life of a French actress who dies from poisoning in the work's closing bars.

The final phase of Italian opera found its most famous exponent in Giacomo Puccini (1858–1924), whose aria 'Nessun Dorma' from *Turandot* must be one of the most widely known operatic excerpts among the general public today.

At the age of 17, Puccini walked 19 miles to attend a performance of Verdi's *Aida*, a work which convinced him that he wanted to write opera. He studied under Ponchielli (among others) at the Milan Conservatory of Music, where he shared a room with Mascagni. He entered the same competition that Mascagni was to win with *Cavalleria Rusticana* but Puccini's entry (**La Villi**) was not ranked. However, his friends helped to pay for it to be staged and it was sufficiently successful for Italy's leading music publisher

Puccini's mature operas

Manon Lescaut, 1893

La bohème, 1896

Tosca, 1900

Madame Butterfly, 1904

La fanciulla del West, 1910

La rondine, 1917

Il trittico, 1918

Turandot, 1926 (posthumous)

to commission a second opera (**Edgar**) from Puccini. It was a failure and was cancelled after only three performances.

Over the years Puccini was to rewrite *Edgar* four times, but he knew that, while the music had many strengths, the plot was weak and the libretto poor. This realisation caused Puccini much angst about the libretto for his next opera, **Manon Lescaut** (1893), which is based on a short novel by the French author Abbé Prévost, first published in 1731. Six writers, one of whom was Leoncavallo (librettist as well as composer of *Pagliacci*) worked on the text before Puccini was satisfied – even his publisher chipped in with some ideas at one stage, as did Puccini himself.

The opera concerns the downfall of Manon, a young woman whose love of luxury leads to her conviction for theft and prostitution. She is sentenced to exile and ends up in a barren wilderness where she dies of thirst in the arms of her lover.

It was a bold choice of subject, as the same novel had already been turned into a successful opera by the French composer Massenet less than ten years earlier. Puccini famously dismissed this as a problem, claiming that Massenet had treated the story as a Frenchman, with powder and minuets, while he would treat it as an Italian, with a desperate passion.

Puccini's *Manon Lescaut* received its premiere in Turin on 1 February 1893, just eight days before the first performance of Verdi's *Falstaff* in Milan. In retrospect, it seemed almost like the older composer handing his baton to the new generation. Puccini's opera gave the composer his first international success. It was also the first of six operas he wrote that feature a flawed heroine who is destined to die.

Manon Lescaut overflows with melodic invention and its rich textures seem, like many works of the 1890s, to be influenced more by Wagner than Verdi. It also reveals how Puccini was developing an ability to paint a mood or suggest a gesture with just a few dabs of instrumental colour.

High points of the work include the intermezzo after Act Two, which is often played as an orchestral work in its own right, and the finale to Act Three. The latter is the embarkation scene in which Manon and other women sentenced to exile are loaded onto a ship. Puccini had many discussions with his librettists on how to structure this scene for best dramatic effect (it was not part of Prevost's novel). The solution they devised was a roll-call of prostitutes and other female criminals by name. To an accompaniment that constantly builds in tension, each is hustled on board – some are defiant, some laugh in contempt, others cover their faces in shame. Meanwhile, crowds on the quayside ominously murmur disapproving or lewd remarks. Over all of this, Manon sings a passionate lament of farewell, joined by her lover who finally persuades the ship's captain to take him on board for the journey.

Despite his difficulties with the librettists for *Manon Lescaut*, Puccini formed a good relationship (at least to the extent that they would produce what he required) with two of them, Illica and Giacosa, and it was they who would write the libretti for Puccini's next three operas: *La bohème*, *Tosca* and *Madame Butterfly*. These three mid-career works, written in succession, form the best-known part of Puccini's output, just as the three mid-career operas written in succession (*Rigoletto*, *Il trovatore* and *La traviata*) occupy a similar place in Verdi's catalogue of works.

featured opera

La bohème (The Bohemians) is loosely based on *Scènes de la vie de bohème* (Scenes of Bohemian life) by the French writer Henri Murger. Originally distributed as a series of short stories and then turned into a play, Murger combined them to form a popular novel first published in 1851. It is a highly romanticised account of the lives of young 'bohemians' – a term referring to impoverished artists, writers, actors and musicians of any nationality – struggling to make a living in the attics of Paris.

Act One starts with a series of amusing vignettes. It is Christmas Eve and the audience is introduced to the remarkably unsuccessful artist Marcello and his friend Rodolfo, who thinks so little of the play he is writing that he burns it in order to try to warm their freezing garret. They are joined by Colline, a philosopher who has failed to pawn some of his books, and then the musician Schaunard, who has unexpectedly earned some money to buy wine. Their landlord arrives to collect the long-overdue rent, so the boys get him drunk to distract him and then decide to go to the Café Momus to blow the rent money on a meal. Rodolfo remains to finish some work when Mimi, a seamstress who lives in a nearby room, calls to ask for a light for her candle. Rodolfo touches her hand in the darkness as they search for the key she dropped, triggering the famous aria, 'Che gelida manima' (Your tiny hand is frozen):

Andantino affettuoso

Che ge - li - da ma - ni - na, se la la - sci ris - cal - der. Cer - car che gio - va?

In fact, this is not just an aria but the start of a highly original Act One finale. The music moves straight into another aria, this time for Mimi in which she gives an account of her modest life. There

Puccini's *La bohème*, 'Che gelida manina'

is no grand ending to this – she tails off into recitative as she worries that it all seems boring. The sounds of the other boys are heard offstage, telling Rodolfo to hurry, and then he sees Mimi bathed in a shaft of moonlight. This is a cue for a passionate duet, based on the two main tunes of 'Che gelida manina' heard in reverse order. They leave together and final exclamations of love (on their topmost notes) are heard in the distance from offstage.

Act Two offers a startling contrast. It is Christmas Eve on a busy Parisian street. The shops are lit by tiny lamps, shop keepers are bawling out their wares in competition with street vendors selling sweets and hot chestnuts. Shoppers are jostling and children add to the commotion. Schaunard is buying a second-hand horn, with an out-of-tune D, and Colline retrieves his overcoat from the pawn shop. Marcello is flirting with some passing girls while Rodolfo buys a new hat for Mimi. He introduces her to his friends and they all sit down at the Café Momus and order a lavish meal.

Marcello's former mistress, Musetta, joins them with Alcindoro, her latest sugar daddy. She takes no notice of his pleas that she is far too loud and that people are staring. In fact, she announces that she wants to be the centre of attention in a lavish and somewhat risqué aria in waltz time:

Tempo di Valzer lento

Quan - do me'n vo' _____ quan - do me'en vo' so - let - ta per la via

Puccini develops Musetta's waltz into an elaborate ensemble in which she flirts with Marcello and then gets Alcindoro out of the way by sending him off to buy her a new pair of shoes. The bohemians find they can't afford the restaurant bill and so they

Puccini's *La bohème*, Musetta's waltz

tell the waiter that Alcindoro will pay as they make a hasty exit. The chaos caused by a passing military parade, led by an onstage *banda*, gives the bohemians a chance to escape through the crowds. Alcindoro collapses in shock when he returns and sees how much he has to pay.

Puccini gives realism – *verismo*, in fact – to the entire act with a wealth of musical detail, ranging from the music sung by children who are pestering their mothers to buy them toys for Christmas, to the way in which the military band at the end of the scene enters in a totally unrelated key, causing just the sort of dislocating effect that so often occurs with street music.

Part of the set for Act Three in Jonathan Miller's production of *La bohème* for English National Opera, which was inspired by photographs of Paris in the 1930s

Act Three sees another striking contrast in scene and mood. It is dawn and snowing on a freezing February morning in the outskirts of the Paris. Again, Puccini paints the scene with precise musical detail. Soft staccato notes played by harp and flute in parallel 5ths give the impression of falling snow flakes while low, sustained notes create a mood of bleak sadness. Offstage voices suggest singing, accompanied by the clinking of glasses, from inside a dingy tavern – even fragments of Musetta's waltz can be heard, so it is clear she is there. Road sweepers and milk sellers go about their business, exchanging brief comments in the icy weather and distant church bells ring for matins.

Mimi comes through the snow to the same melody that announced her arrival in Act One, but this time it is obscured by her violent fit of coughing. She has come to find Rodolfo, who has abandoned her. He is sleeping in the tavern where Marcello and Musetta now board. She hides when Rodolfo appears and overhears him tell Marcello the real reason why he left – he fears that Mimi is dying from consumption (tuberculosis). He has no money to help her and so Rodolfo hopes that by pretending indifference she will leave him and find a wealthier suitor. Then he sees her and they embrace. The act ends with a quartet in which Rodolfo and Mimi agree that they must part, but not before spring arrives, while at the same time Marcello and Musetta hurl abuse at each other as she walks out on the artist with immediate effect.

The final act is set in the same attic room as Act One. Spring has come and Marcello and Rodolfo both miss their absent sweethearts. The four boys are as poor as ever, but now their forced humour seems like a ghostly mirror of their gaiety in Act One. As their pretence at dancing turns into a mock duel the door suddenly flies open. Musetta is there with Mimi, who is in a dreadful state, close to death. Mimi begs Rodolfo to be allowed to spend her last moments with him. The other bohemians leave to raise whatever they can to pay for treatment – Colline even re-pawns his overcoat. Left alone, Mimi and Rodolfo relive the happiness of their first meeting and the music associated with it. The others return. Musetta has sold her earrings to pay for medicine and has bought a fur muff so that Mimi's tiny hand need no longer be frozen. They tell Rodolfo that a doctor has been called.

Schaunard tiptoes to Mimi's bed and then whispers to Marcello that it is too late, she has died. They watch helplessly as Rodolfo proclaims that he still has hope and tries to shield Mimi from a ray of sunshine that has lit her face. Suddenly he notices the ashen faces of his friends and, unable to sing, asks in speaking tone why they have such strange looks. Marcello hugs him and simply utters 'poor fellow'. At last realising what has happened, Rodolfo screams 'Mimi, Mimi' and falls sobbing over her dead body. Musetta and Marcello are in tears and the remaining bohemians are numbed in their grief. Despite a veneer of Romantic sentimentality in the work, verismo turns its knife into the audience at the very last, just before they leave the theatre.

In fact, the nature of verismo in opera was always quite fluid and in La bohème it is evident more in the portrayal of the lives of the poor and the overwhelming sadness and intimacy of Mimi's death than in scenes of violence. Also typical of verismo opera, and especially of Puccini, is the highly charged musical style and the extreme contrasts devised to heighten the emotional impact of the work.

Although the music is continuous throughout each of the four acts of La bohème, the underlying structure of arias, duets and ensembles is still evident. However, these focal points are interspersed with particularly natural settings of dialogue between the characters, most of whom also have distinctive musical motives that are woven into the fabric of the opera.

La bohème has, for many years, been one of the most frequently performed works in the world of professional opera, although its popularity ranking is often challenged by Puccini's next work for the stage.

News of Puccini's intention to write an opera on the subject of **Tosca** had been leaked to the press in 1889, eleven years before its premiere in 1900. The work was to be based on a play, *La Tosca*, by the French dramatist Victorien Sardou and written for the most famous actress of her day, Sarah Bernhardt. It was first staged in 1887. Again it took several years of negotiation with his librettists before Puccini was satisfied with the text. He was concerned with the dramatic impact of every word, for instance pointing out how the exclamation 'How you hate me!' is so much more effective than the questioning 'Do you hate me?'. Unlike *La bohème*, *Tosca* was to be blood-and-thunder *verismo* with torture, corruption, lust and four deaths.

The drama is set in three locations that still exist in Rome today and it condenses the events of an 18-hour time span into a period of just under two hours. Act One takes place in the church of Sant' Andrea della Valle during the day of 17 June 1800. Act Two takes place that same evening in the nearby Palazzo Farnese, and Act Three takes place at dawn the next morning on the roof of the Castel Sant' Angelo which stands high above the River Tiber, near the Vatican.

The precise date is known because it had taken three days for news to reach Rome of the Battle of Marengo, a real event that took place on 14 June in Northern Italy. The change in Napoleon's fortunes at that battle forms a key element in the plot.

In Act One the artist Cavaradossi is working in a church on his painting of Mary Magdalene. He contrasts the beauty of the blonde woman he has painted with the dark beauty of his jealous mistress, the opera singer Floria Tosca:

The lilting melody of this ternary-form song and its brevity are typical of Puccini's most popular solos, while the church sacristan's disapproving mutterings in the background add a touch of *verismo* to this set-piece aria.

Puccini's *Tosca*, Cavaradossi's aria

Cavaradossi supports Napoleon's cause and he helps an escaped political prisoner to hide in his villa. While he is gone, news arrives that Napoleon has been defeated.

There will be a grand celebration in church and the choir leap and shout for joy at the prospect of double pay. The scene is a foil for the entry of Scarpia, the villainous chief of police, who suddenly appears to the sound of three thunderous chords – a motif heard at the start of the opera and associated with him throughout the work.

Scarpia is on the track of Angelotti, an escaped political prisoner. He has calculated that he can use Tosca to crack the resolve of Cavaradossi, who he believes is shielding Angelotti.

Another of Puccini's highly original finales begins with Scarpia ordering three agents to take a carriage and follow Tosca. The finale takes the form of a long crescendo underpinned by the sound of distant church bells playing a restless *ostinato* for more than 70 bars. As more and more instruments join in, the church starts to fill with worshippers. The sound of an offstage canon is heard at intervals, indicating that a prisoner has escaped. Smaller bells begin to beat faster patterns and a church organ heralds the start of a huge religious procession. Priests and congregation recite spoken prayers in rhythm, above which Scarpia sings of his lust for Tosca – his double target is to see the painter Cavaradossi dead and Tosca in his own arms. The finale reaches its climax as everyone begins singing a Te Deum in celebration of Napoleon's victory, supported by onstage brass, but cut short by the orchestra in the pit which ends the act with three statements of Scarpia's chilling motif.

Act Two opens with Scarpia in his apartment in the Farnese Palace. When he opens a window the sound of a concert is heard in the gardens – offstage instruments playing a gavotte, and then an offstage choir accompanying Tosca in a cantata. As she sings, Scarpia's agents arrive on stage. They have not found Angelotti but Cavaradossi, who is not co-operating, is dragged in. Tosca is summoned and Cavaradossi just has time to tell her to say nothing before he is dragged away to an adjacent room for torture. Tosca is at first defiant, but the sound of her lover's screams breaks her resolve and she reveals Angelotti's hiding place to Scarpia.

Cavaradossi is dragged back in a terrible state, but revives when he hears the news that Napoleon has not lost – he rallied his troops, counter-attacked and won. Scarpia sends his agent to find Angelotti and orders Cavaradossi to be imprisoned. Then Scarpia gives Tosca the choice of sleeping with him or watching Cavaradossi die. In the aria 'Vissi d'Arte' she wonders why God allows her to suffer when she has only lived to serve her art. Scarpia's agent returns with the news that Angelotti has committed suicide.

Tosca agrees to Scarpia's lustful demands in return for a pass to leave Rome safely with Cavaradossi. For the sake of appearances Scarpia says there will have to be a

The finale to Act One of *Tosca* (English National Opera)

mock execution but the firing squad will use blanks, as they did on a similar occasion. After he has signed the pass, Scarpia sings 'Tosca, at last you are mine' and rises to embrace her, but she retorts 'This is Tosca's kiss' as she kills him with a knife she has hidden. Wiping the blood from her hands, she pulls the pass from Scarpia's clenched fingers and scornfully sings 'And before him, all Rome trembled!'.

After an opening flourish, Act Three begins with an extended musical impression of Rome just before dawn. A shepherd boy is heard singing a faux folksong offstage as he drives his flock through the streets, oblivious to the tragedy about to occur.

Then a string melody slowly unwinds to the accompaniment of numerous bells played in different locations in the theatre and intended to recreate the sound of the churches of Rome summoning the faithful to the first services of the day. Puccini went to enormous trouble to get the effect right, even sleeping in the Castel Sant' Angelo to be ready to check the tone, pitch, distance and pattern of each

The importance that Puccini placed on realism (*verismo*) in *Tosca* is reflected in the research he undertook to find the precise vestments and liturgy that would have been used for a service in Sant' Andrea della Valle in 1800, in finding dialect words for the song of the shepherd boy at the start of Act Three, and in recording exactly how the bells of Rome sounded from the roof of the Castel Sant' Angelo for the music that follows this song.

set of church bells. He then had suitable bells specially cast for the first production of *Tosca* (which took place in Rome).

At length, the prisoner Cavaradossi is led in. He asks to be left alone to write a last letter to his beloved, but is overcome with memories of her in the aria 'E lucevan le stelle' (When the stars were shining brightly).

Suddenly Tosca arrives with the safe-conduct pass and confesses to Cavaradossi that she has murdered Scarpia. She relays the instructions about the mock execution and adds that Cavaradossi must fall convincingly when he hears the shots, just like Tosca acting a part in an opera.

A bell strikes 4 o'clock and the firing squad enter to an ominous measured tread. They take aim, fire their rifles, and Cavaradossi falls. Tosca waits an age for them to leave before running to her lover and telling him to get up. He doesn't move when she shakes him and Tosca then sees that her hands are covered in blood. Scarpia has not kept his word and Cavaradossi is dead.

Immediately sounds of shouting are heard as men rush up to the roof of the Castel Sant' Angelo. Scarpia's body has been found and his agents rush in to arrest Tosca. She climbs to the castle parapet and, with a cry that she will meet Scarpia before God, Tosca leaps to her death.

The premiere of *Tosca* took place at La Scala, Milan, on 17 March 1900 and was highly successful. That summer Puccini travelled to England for the triumphant first performance of the work at Covent Garden. While in London, he saw a one-act play entitled *Madame Butterfly*, based on a short story of 1898 by an American lawyer named John Luther Long. Puccini had found the basis for his next opera.

With a libretto by the familiar team of Illica and Giacosa, **Madame Butterfly** was first staged in 1904, again at La Scala, Milan. It is an example of western fascination with oriental culture that had begun with the display of Japanese art at the Paris Exposition Universelle in 1867 and that had been parodied in the Gilbert and Sullivan operetta, *The Mikado,* of 1885 and the English musical comedy of 1896 *The Geisha* by Sidney Jones. Even closer to Puccini's work, and probably used as an additional source by his librettists, was *Madame Chrysanthème*, a French novel of 1887 turned into a now forgotten comic opera. For information about authentic Japanese melodies used by Puccini in the opera see http://daisyfield.com/music/jpm/Puccini.htm.

Madame Butterfly tells the tragedy of a young Japanese girl who is seduced by Lieutenant Pinkerton, an American naval officer. Against the advice of the American consul, he is 'temporarily wedded' to her while he remains in port, according to Japanese custom of the day. When his ship sails, he leaves her, promising to return 'when the robins rebuild their nest'.

Butterfly has Pinkerton's baby, three years pass, her family have deserted her, but in the aria 'Un bel dì' she still clings to the hope that he will return one fine day. When that day comes, he returns with his American wife and Butterfly at last realises what has happened. She says farewell to her little boy, blindfolds him and gives him a tiny American flag with which to greet his father. She then goes behind a screen where she kills herself with a knife. Pinkerton and the consul arrive too later to save her.

The first performance of *Madame Butterfly* was a catastrophe. This may in part have been due to the work being finished late and inadequately rehearsed, but it seems it was mainly the result of a vendetta against the opera by a rival publisher. Nevertheless, Puccini made some changes to the work before it was performed again, much more successfully, a few months later. He then made further revisions for the opera's premieres in London and Paris, the latter being the version usually performed today.

The more reflective nature of *Madame Butterfly* is very different from the continuous dramatic action of *Tosca*, but it soon became very popular with the public. Puccini is also said to have preferred it to any of his other operas, perhaps because the nature of the subject freed him to explore textures, harmonies and colours that are more exotic than those he had used before.

The stage play of *Madame Butterfly* that Puccini had seen in London had been adapted from John Luther Long's original short story by an American writer named David Bellasco. It was to Bellasco's own play, *The Girl of the Golden West,* that Puccini turned for his next opera, **La fanciulla del West** (1910). It tells the story of how Minnie, the no-nonsense girl who runs a saloon for the rough and desperate gold prospectors of California, wins their hearts and teaches them the virtues of hope, forgiveness and compassion.

The work was commissioned by the Metropolitan Opera in New York, where two of the most famous singers of the age, Enrico Caruso and Emmy Destinn, took the leading roles in the first performance. Arturo Toscanini, who had been entrusted with the first performances of *La Bohème* and Leoncavallo's *Pagliacci*, conducted.

Puccini's next opera, **La rondine** (The Swallow) was not performed until 1917, delayed in part by the outbreak of the First World War. It had a favourable premiere in Monte Carlo and is the composer's only full-length comic opera, but it has never been popular enough to find a permanent place in operatic repertoire.

The success of *Cavalleria rusticana* and *Pagliacci*, had long given Puccini the desire to write works of similar length. Initially he thought of pairing a tragedy with a comedy, but eventually he decided to include a third opera, a work of religious mysticism. All three deal with the subject of deception and were intended to be performed together as one evening's entertainment, under the title **Il trittico** (The Triptych, 1918). Each lasts for less than an hour, so *Il trittico* is like a three-act opera with two intervals, except that its three parts are unrelated and highly contrasting.

The first opera is **Il tabarro** (The Cloak), based on a one-act play by Didier Gold in the French dramatic horror tradition known as *Grand Guignol*. Puccini's operatic version is among the last examples of classic, violent *verismo*.

The skipper of a barge on the river Seine suspects that his wife is having an affair with a member of his crew. He is right, but when the young man sees a light from the barge he mistakes it as a signal to visit her, only to encounter the skipper who forces him to confess, strangles him and then hides the body under a cloak. When the skipper's wife returns and asks for shelter from the cold night air, he opens the cloak to reveal the lifeless body of her lover, and pushes her face against his dead lips in retribution.

The second opera **Suor Angelica** (Sister Angelica) could not be more different. Whereas *Il tabarro* is set in the working-class Paris of 1910, *Suor Angelica* is an original story set in a 17th-century Italian convent. Angelica was sent there by her noble family after she gave birth to an illegitimate child. Her aunt arrives to tell her that the child has died and, in despair, the niece takes poison. Realising that suicide is a mortal sin, she prays for mercy to the Virgin Mary who appears in a vision with her child and leads the dying nun to heaven.

The third opera is **Gianni Schicchi,** a comedy set in 13th-century Florence with a libretto based on an incident in Dante's *Divine Comedy*, written in the early years of the 14th century. Buoso Donati has died and his avaricious relatives are horrified to learn that he has left his considerable wealth to a monastery.

They call for the wily Gianni Schicchi, who suggests that since nobody outside the family knows the old man is dead, he should get into bed, pretend to be Donati and write a new will. There are narrow squeaks when a doctor calls to give the patient an enema, and when the funeral bell starts tolling at the local church (which turns out to be for someone else). In the meantime, some of the more unscrupulous relatives try to steal the silver.

Eventually a lawyer arrives who warns that the penalty for falsifying a will, or even being an accomplice, is to have a hand chopped off and be exiled. Schicchi, pretending to be Donati, dictates the new will but to the dismay of the relatives, he bequeaths most of the estate to himself. Schicchi reminds the family of the need to keep quiet by periodically waving a hand from beneath the bedclothes and singing 'goodbye Florence'. Eventually he drives all of the relatives out of what is now his house, apart from his daughter and a young man from the Donati family with whom she is in love. Schicchi can now afford her dowry, and he asks the audience to agree that no better use could have been found for Donati's legacy.

Il trittico was first staged in New York where it was generally well received. Of the three operas, which are now not always performed together as Puccini had intended, *Gianni Schicchi* has proved the most popular, while *Suor Angelica* can seem rather sentimental without a strong cast and firm direction.

Puccini's last opera, **Turandot**, is based on what was probably an ancient Arabian folk tale. This formed the basis of a play by Carlo Gozzi in 1762, which was totally reworked by Puccini's librettists. The beautiful but icy Princess Turandot lives in ancient China and has sworn that, as revenge for the rape of one of her ancestors, no man will ever possess her. By way of protection she has taken an oath that any suitor must solve three riddles. Failure results in death, as many have discovered.

However, when Prince Calaf passes the test, Turandot pleads with her father, the Emperor of China, to release her from the vow. He will not, but Calaf offers her a way out by agreeing to die if Turandot can guess his real name by dawn. The entire city of Peking is kept awake on the task of finding it, as Calaf reflects in the famous aria 'Nessun dorma' (None shall sleep). Calaf's blind father is tortured and the girl who has helped him commits suicide when she realises that her love for Calaf will never be returned. The prince is so moved by this gesture that he tells Turandot his name, thereby risking his own death. However, he has melted her icy heart and she embraces him, telling the people of Peking that Calaf's name is love.

Puccini died before finishing the opera, which was completed by the composer Franco Alfano, based partially on some of Puccini's sketches, and first performed in 1926. *Turandot* has become a much loved and frequently performed work. However, it also proved to be the last Italian opera to form part of mainstream operatic repertoire, after Italy's dominance in the field for more than 300 years.

Salle Le Peletier, home of the Paris *Opéra* from 1821 to 1873

France

The late-18th-century vogue for 'rescue operas' in Paris has already been discussed (see page 68). Perhaps the most famous of such works was ***Richard Coeur-de-lion*** (Richard the Lionheart, 1784) by André Grétry (1741–1813). It is a type of work known as ***opéra comique***, which does not mean a humorous work but rather an opera in which the dialogue between the musical numbers is spoken rather than sung as recitative.

Other early composers of *opéra comique* include the Italian-born Luigi Cherubini (1760–1842), Étienne Méhul (1763–1817) and François-Adrien Boieldieu (1775–1834), the last of whom introduced a lighter style to *opéra comique*.

Following the French revolution of 1789 there was a short-lived glut of works designed to celebrate the new republic and spread its political philosophy, such as ***Le triomphe de la République*** (The Triumph of the Republic, 1793) by François-Joseph Gossec (1734–1829). It features folk tunes and popular dances as if to disassociate itself deliberately from pre-revolutionary court opera.

By the start of the 19th century, Napoleon had reduced the proliferating number of opera houses in Paris to the Opéra-Comique and the Opéra, the latter being for serious works without spoken dialogue. In addition, the Théâtre-Italien catered for those who wanted to see popular *opere buffe* and the latest operas in *bel canto* style coming out of Italy.

At the Opéra, composers such as the Italian-born Gaspare Spontini (1774–1851) developed the traditions of Gluck reform opera for contemporary taste, particularly in his most famous work, **La Vestale** (The Vestal Virgins, 1807).

Grand opera and *Opéra comique*

In 1821 the Paris Opéra moved into a large new theatre on the rue Le Peletier which was superbly equipped for the stage works of the day. In 1822 it became the first opera house to use gas lighting rather than oil lamps and candles. A few years later it introduced limelight – an intense type of lighting produced by heating a cylinder of quicklime with a very hot flame. It was used to illuminate soloists and is still remembered in the

> The new Paris Opéra could seat 1900 people and it housed an orchestra of more than 80. There was a chorus of nearly 80 singers and up to 80 non-singing extras were available. There were 60 stage hands for moving scenery and working special effects.

expression 'to be in the limelight'. In 1849 the theatre was almost certainly the first to employ electricity when it used an arc lamp to simulate a sunrise (see overleaf). It was also well equipped with the latest stage machinery and was the first opera house to appoint a stage manager to supervise the large stage crew.

The magnificent facilities of this new theatre, as well as the money provided by its sponsorship from the state, helped to establish the type of work known as grand opera. Characterised by large ensembles, lavish stage designs and often spectacular special effects, grand operas most commonly have four or five acts, with a plot that sets romantic passions against historical strife, and they generally include a sequence of ballet dances that sometimes have only a tenuous link with the plot. The use of spectacle and dance were, of course, features that can be traced back to the very earliest French operas.

The first grand opera was **La muette de Portici** (The mute girl of Portici, 1828) by Daniel Auber (1782–1871). It shows its grand opera credentials by ending with a volcanic eruption of Mount Vesuvius as the background to a fearsome battle.

The resources and finance available in Paris proved to be a magnet for Italian composers, and 1829 saw the premiere of Rossini's last, and only, grand opera, *Guillaume Tell* (William Tell). Later, Verdi's grand operas *Les vêpres siciliennes* and *Don Carlos* were both originally conceived for Paris, and he turned *Il trovatore* into a French-language grand opera, adding the obligatory ballet sequence in the process. *Aida* is also a grand opera, even though written for Cairo.

The Paris Opéra also attracted German composers, such as Giacomo Meyerbeer (1791–1864) who was one of the most famous opera composers of his day, although his works are now seldom performed. His first grand opera was **Robert le diable** (Robert the Devil, 1831). It tells the tale of a struggle between good and evil, and the dangers of dabbling with the supernatural, ending in truly spectacular fashion with the devil being swallowed up in an earthquake. Its ballet sequence scandalised Paris by depicting the ghosts of debauched nuns rising from their graves and being led by their abbess to do the work of Satan.

Meyerbeer's **Les Huguenots** tells the story of the St Bartholomew's Day massacre of 1572, in which thousands of Protestants were murdered by Catholics in Paris and the surrounding areas. It created a sensation when first performed in 1836 with its huge crowd scenes, large orchestra (which includes six harps and the recently invented bass clarinet, as well as onstage wind groups), nuns' chorus, gypsy ballet and water ballet (danced by young ladies in gauze bathing costumes in the first production, although Meyerbeer complained that it was difficult to see them).

Despite requiring a large number of soloists, there are few arias in *Les Huguenots* as Meyerbeer has a preference for elaborate ensemble scenes. Costumes and scenery at the premiere were lavish. The fifth act alone requires three different sets with transformations between each of them. The last of these is a full-depth scene of Paris at night, illuminated by soldiers with torches pursuing the fleeing Protestants, crying out 'Dieu veut le sang!' (God wants blood!) as the curtain comes down on a scene of total carnage.

Almost as popular in its day was Meyerbeer's **Le Prophète** (The Prophet, 1849), which has the unusual distinction of being the first opera to include roller-skating, the latest craze in Paris at the time, in a ballet intended to portray skating on a frozen lake. It was also the first opera production to make use of electricity, in order to create the effect of a sunrise, as mentioned earlier. Maintaining the grand opera tradition of spectacular finales, the work ends with a royal palace being blown up and collapsing on its occupants.

Hector Berlioz (1803–1869) was the most original of his generation of French composers and one of the greatest experts on orchestration. However, his attitude to Meyerbeer's music was ambivalent. He found things to praise in the older composer's work, particularly his use of instruments, but Berlioz became very critical of what he came to see as the commercialism of Meyerbeer's style.

The death of Dido from Act 5 of the first production of *Les Troyens* by Berlioz in 1863

Perhaps there was an element of jealousy in this, since Meyerbeer was extremely popular while Berlioz found it very difficult to get the small number of operas he completed to the stage.

Berlioz abandoned his first opera, **Les francs-juges** (The judges of the secret court, 1826) after it became obvious that he could not get it staged. Its very fine overture has become a much-loved concert piece, but Berlioz subsequently destroyed much of the rest of the work.

Benvenuto Cellini started life as a two-act opéra comique (with spoken dialogue) about the eventful life of a 16th-century Italian. The Paris Opéra-Comique thought the work too serious for its repertoire and so, after Berlioz had reworked the piece to remove the spoken dialogue, it was staged at the Paris Opéra in 1838. The result was a disaster. Berlioz recorded that the audience hissed 'with admirable energy and unanimity' and the musicians declared the work to be unperformable. They weren't entirely right, but the opera is very challenging and modern performances are rare. However, once again the overture has remained popular, and Berlioz salvaged some of the rest of the music to form one of his best-known concert overtures known as *Le carnaval romain* (The Roman Carnival).

Mephistopheles and Faust in Terry Gilliam's 2011 production of *The Damnation of Faust* for English National Opera

After another unfinished opera, Berlioz embarked on his most ambitious project, **Les Troyens** (The Trojans), with a libretto that he wrote himself, based on Virgil's epic poem, *The Aeneid*. Berlioz wrote the work as a grand opera in five acts. It was conceived on a large scale and the only suitable venue was the Paris Opéra who were reluctant to stage such a long and complex work. After five years of unproductive negotiations, Berlioz agreed to let the much smaller Théâtre Lyrique present a cut-down version of the second half of the opera, which retells the story of Dido and Aeneas (see page 45). Although Berlioz was unhappy with the standard of performance, the work was well received by other musicians. However, the composer never lived to see the first two acts performed and it was not until the 20th century that *Les Troyens* was staged in its entirety in a single evening, as Berlioz had intended.

Berlioz's last opera was **Béatrice et Bénédict**, for which he again wrote his own libretto, based on Shakespeare's *Much Ado About Nothing*. The work is in two acts and its premiere took place in Germany in 1862. The first Parisian performance, at the Opéra-Comique, didn't take place until 1890, long after the composer's death, and the work has never been widely popular, although performances are becoming more frequent in the 21st century.

There is one other work by Berlioz that is sometimes staged today. *La damnation de Faust* (The Damnation of Faust) was written as a concert work and first performed at the Opéra-Comique in 1846. It is written for four solo voices, chorus, children's choir and orchestra. Berlioz originally called it a 'concert opera' although he later changed the description to *légende dramatique* (dramatic legend). It was not a great success, possibly because the audience didn't take to its hybrid form, which seemed to be neither opera nor oratorio. In modern times, fully staged performances have proved successful, despite its relative lack of continuous narrative and its inclusion of lengthy instrumental sections.

The legend of Faust selling his soul to the Devil (in the form of Mephistopheles) in exchange for unlimited knowledge and worldly pleasures appealed to many 19th-century composers. The original version of **Faust** by Charles Gounod (1818–1893) had the five acts of grand opera but no ballet or recitative (the dialogue was spoken, as in *opéra comique*). It was first performed in 1859 at the Théâtre Lyrique which by now had become the fourth opera house in Paris. This type of hybrid between *opéra* and *opéra comique* became known as **opéra lyrique** after the name of the theatre in which it had been encouraged.

Faust took a few years to become really successful, but by 1869 it was playing at the Opéra itself, in a revised version that includes recitative with orchestral accompaniment and the obligatory 15-minute ballet sequence. The latter consists of seven jolly dances that are often played in concerts as 'The ballet music from *Faust*', but as they have only a very tenuous link with the plot, this scene is now often omitted from productions of the opera.

Gounod's *Faust* has very little of the dramatic struggle between good and evil that forms the core of the great play about Faust by the German author Goethe, to which Gounod's opera is very distantly related. Gounod's popularity came from his ability to write a long succession of memorable, toe-tapping melodies, including the flower song, the jewel song and the soldiers' chorus:

Gounod's *Faust*,
Soldiers' Chorus

Tempo di marcia

pp

Of Gounod's 12 completed operas, the only other still occasionally performed today is **Roméo et Juliette** (1867), based on Shakespeare's play. It is another opéra lyrique, and is famed for its five duets for the doomed, eponymous lovers.

A fascination with the orient has already been seen in operas such as Mozart's *The abduction from the Seraglio* and Rossini's *The Italian Girl in Algiers*. A new enthusiasm for the colour, exoticism and perceived sensuality of the east developed in Paris during the second half of the 19th century, and helped fire enthusiasm for works such Verdi's *Aida* (1871), set in ancient Egypt.

Meyerbeer's last grand opera, first performed in 1865 shortly after his death, was **L'Africaine** which, despite its title, is about an Indian princess. The subject of **Lakmé** (1883) by Léo Delibes (1836–1891) is an Indian priestess, whose 'Flower duet' with her servant, 'Sous le dôme épais' (Under the dense canopy) remains the opera's most famous number.

In 1863, a young and little known composer Georges Bizet (1838–1875) achieved some success with the public, although not with the press, for his latest opera. **Les pêcheurs de perles** (The Pearl Fishers) was first played at the Théâtre Lyrique and follows the passion of the day for exotic locations by being set in Ceylon (now Sri Lanka). Although the work is uneven in quality, it is still occasionally performed today, and is another opera particularly remembered for a duet, this time for tenor and baritone, 'Au fond du temple saint' (At the back of the holy temple) in which the two friends fondly recall both falling in love with the same priestess.

Bizet achieved few successes in his short life and even his final opera was not well received at first. Sadly, he never lived to see **Carmen** become one of the most popular and frequently performed works in the entire operatic repertoire.

featured opera

Carmen was written as an *opéra comique* (with spoken dialogue) in four acts and was first performed at the Opéra-Comique in Paris, on 3 March 1875. The libretto by Henri Meilhac and Ludovic Halévy is based on a short story of the same name by Prosper Mérimée, first published in 1845.

The work begins with a prelude, which is actually a pot-pourri overture that gives a preview of the music for the entry of the bullfighters from Act Three, the chorus of the Toreador's song from Act Two and a sinister motif that will be associated with the fate of Carmen as the opera unfolds.

Act One is set in a square in Seville in the hot south of Spain. A group of soldiers waiting for a change of guard passes the time by commenting on the passers-by. A bugle call from offstage is answered by a bugle call onstage. Then a boys' choir, dressed as street urchins, sings about playing soldiers while the real guard is changed. Their

A scene from *Carmen* at Glyndebourne Opera House

corporal, Don José, has just missed seeing his girlfriend, Micaëla, when the girls in a cigarette factory come out for a break. The last to emerge is Carmen, the girl with gypsy blood. She enters to a fast version of the fate motif and then sings that 'Love is a rebellious bird that nobody can tame':

The sinuously descending chromatic line of the melody perfectly characterises the seductive Carmen, while the repeating bass rhythm identifies the song as a habanera — a popular dance style from Cuba. However, although this is the most famous aria in *Carmen*, it is not by Bizet! He thought he was quoting a Spanish folksong, but in fact the source of the music that he had adapted

Bizet's *Carmen*, 'Love is a rebellious bird that nobody can tame' (habanera)

was a song by the Spanish composer Sebastián Yradier, published only a few years earlier. Yradier was acknowledged in the score as the composer of this number, once the error had been noticed.

Carmen tosses a flower to Don José, but then Micaëla arrives with a letter from his mother who thinks it is time for him to leave the army and marry Micaëla. The cigarette girls suddenly rush out of the factory. The tempestuous Carmen has attacked one of them with a knife, for which she is arrested and placed in the charge of Don José, but she soon uses her charms to persuade him to free her.

Act Two is set in Lillas Pastia's inn and begins with a fiery gypsy dance. Time has passed and Carmen is pleased to hear that Don José has been freed after serving a short sentence for letting her escape. The noise of a crowd is heard offstage. They are welcoming the bullfighter Escamillo, who sings in praise of his calling:

In the score Bizet described the Toreador's song as **couplets,** a term used in France for a song in a popular style that forms a self-standing number in *opéra comique.* Many *couplets,* like this one, are in strophic form with a refrain.

Bizet's *Carmen,*
Toreador's song

Escamillo tries to flirt with Carmen, but she is waiting for Don José. After the crowds have left the inn, two gypsy girls plan a smuggling escapade with their boyfriends but, in a lively quintet, Carmen says she will not go with them. Don José at last arrives and Carmen dances for him, playing castanets to accompany her steps. Offstage trumpet calls are superimposed upon the end of her song – a signal that Don José must return to barracks. Before he can leave, his commanding officer arrives and they fight over Carmen. Having drawn his sword on an officer, Don José cannot return to the army and has no choice but to join Carmen and the smugglers.

Act Three is set in a camp in the mountains. Carmen has become bored with Don José and tells him to go back to his mother. The gypsy girls pass the time by reading their fortune in the cards. As the fate motif sounds its warning from the orchestra, Carmen turns the cards and sees them foretell death. Escamillo, the bullfighter, arrives at the camp, announcing that he has come for Carmen. He and Don José fight over her with knives. Escamillo's knife breaks and Carmen saves his life by restraining Don José. Tempers calm, and Escamillo invites everyone to his next bullfight. The faithful Micaëla has come in fear of her life to tell Don José that his mother is dying. He vows that he will return to Carmen, after which Escamillo is heard offstage, as if from afar, singing snatches of the Toreador's song as the act comes to an end.

Act Four is set outside the bullring in Seville and begins with a vivid scene of street vendors selling programmes, refreshments, cigarettes and souvenirs to the gathering crowds. Children and adults hail the parade of bullfighters, led by Escamillo and Carmen. Escamillo goes on into the ring with the crowds, but Carmen stays outside after being warned that Don José is nearby. He implores her to return to him, while offstage cheers and fanfares for Escamillo are heard from within the bullring. As the fate motif thunders out from the orchestra, Carmen repeatedly refuses to go with Don José and she throws his ring back at him. In fury, he retorts 'Well then, you are damned' and stabs her to death with his knife. As the crowds come surging out of the bullring, praising Escamillo, the fate motif turns from minor to major, Don José confesses that he has killed the woman he loved, and the curtain falls rapidly as he is arrested.

Each act of *Carmen* is preceded by a piece of instrumental music. There is the prelude before Act One, of course, and then a rather martial **entr'acte** before Act Two that perhaps suggests Don José's time under military arrest. He sings the melody of this *entr'acte* from offstage when he makes his next entry, halfway through Act Two. The *entr'acte* before Act Three had originally been intended for a different work by Bizet. It starts with a long and elegant melody for flute accompanied by harp, and is often performed outside the opera as a short concert work. The final *entr'acte* before Act Four is a fast, surging movement that conjures up the sultry passion that dominates the short final act. It gets its strongly Spanish flavour from being loosely based on a piece from a little-known Spanish opera of 1804, but Bizet adds in a lot of his own material, and intensifies the mood with a lively orchestration, including the characteristic sound of the tambourine.

The initially poor reception of *Carmen*, now one of the world's most popular operas, may seem surprising. After all, with most of the action taking place in the seemingly foreign world of gypsies, it reflects the exoticism that was still in vogue in opera, even if the location is Spain rather than the mysterious orient.

In fact, the reviews of the first performance make it clear that a major objection was to the way that women were being portrayed on the stage at this time. In particular, reviewers referred with considerable disgust to the subject of *Carmen* as a love affair between 'two odious beings' – 'a fallen woman and a deserter'.

Audiences were equally alarmed to discover that what they might have expected to be a charming lyric opera turned out to be a work that began with working-class girls employed in a cigarette factory and ended with the leading lady being stabbed to death and her leading man being arrested.

Of course, what they had all stumbled into was the type of gritty realism that would later become known as *verismo*, but some 15 years ahead of its time. Indeed, one of the few positive reviews of the work congratulated Bizet for 'showing real men and real women, dazzled, tortured by passion'. It did not take long for countries other than France to appreciate the worth of *Carmen*, even though Bizet did not live to see this. Within ten years, his last opera was starting to enter the permanent repertoire of every opera company around the world.

> Shortly before his death, Bizet agreed to *Carmen* being turned into a grand opera for a production at the Vienna Court Opera. The task of setting the spoken dialogue into orchestrally accompanied recitative and adding a ballet (using music from an earlier work by Bizet) was undertaken by Bizet's friend and fellow composer, Ernest Guiraud. For most of the next century, opera houses used this version, or a hybrid one that retained part of the spoken dialogue and used only some of Guirard's recitatives. In recent decades, there has been a tendency to prefer the original *opéra lyrique* version of *Carmen*, despite the fact that it requires singers to tackle extended passages of spoken French.

One of the best-known French composers of the late-Romantic period was Camille Saint-Saëns (1835–1921). Although he wrote more than a dozen operas, the only one that is still performed with any frequency today is **Samson et Dalila** (1877), a grand opera in three acts. Although it is based on the biblical story of Samson and Delilah, it includes a scene in which Delilah tries to seduce Samson into revealing the secret of his strength. It features the beautiful song 'Mon cœur s'ouvre à ta voix' ('My heart opens itself to your voice', usually known in English as 'Softly awakes my heart'), in which an ecstatic Samson moans 'Delilah, Delilah, I love you' after the first verse, before joining in full duet for the end of the second verse.

Even more worldly is the opera's ballet sequence, a **Bacchanale** for the Philistines, for which Saint-Saëns supplies an oriental-sounding melody over wild war drums:

Samson et Dalila is an indication that Parisian opera-goers in 1877 still had a taste for the exotic and oriental, a view that is supported by the subject of another opera from the same year. *Le roi de Lahore* (The King of Lahore) is a grand opera in five

Saint-Saëns's *Samson et Dalila*, Bacchanale

acts and was the first major operatic success for Jules Massenet (1842–1912).

An enormously prolific composer who wrote more than 30 operas, Massenet is now chiefly remembered for **Manon** (1884). This is a gentler and more elegant approach to the novel that also forms the basis of the much more passionate opera by Puccini, *Manon Lescaut*, first staged only a few years later in 1893 (see page 94). Both operas are still performed fairly frequently today. Massenet's **Werther** (1892), loosely based on a semi-autobiographical novel by Goethe, also remains popular, despite (or perhaps because of) its almost unbearably sentimental story of Charlotte, whose jilted lover shoots himself on Christmas Eve while her younger siblings sing Christmas carols outside the window.

The story of French Romantic opera effectively comes to an end in 1900, with the premiere of **Louise** by Gustave Charpentier (1860–1956). Like *La bohème*, the work is set in Paris and tells the story of a seamstress who falls in love with an artist. It is tempting to assume that Charpentier, who wrote the libretto as well as the music, based his ideas on Puccini's opera, but he had in fact started work on *Louise* some years before the premiere of *La bohème* in 1896. *Louise* is very different in that the city of Paris, represented by its authentic street cries that permeate much of the work, is treated almost like a character in the drama. Its scenes, pleasures, mysteries and traditions are central to the plot, and it is Paris that is blamed in the dénouement, when a father loses his daughter to the city.

Louise, is a very atmospheric work and it includes many details of domestic life in Paris and even examples of local dialect in the text. It is, in fact, a rare example of French *verismo*. The work was given further realism by the use of an entirely prose libretto – something that would be increasingly common in the 20th century. It was an immediate success when first produced, but the work requires a very large cast, and today performances of *Louise* are rare.

Long before *Louise* was first performed, a young composer called Debussy had begun work on **Pelléas et Mélisande**, a work that would make a fundamental break with the traditions of the Romantic opera. But that is a topic for the next chapter.

Germany: Weber and Wagner

At the end of the last chapter, Mozart's transformation of the humble *Singspiel* into a work that combined some of the best features of both *opera seria* and *opera buffa* was described.

Singspiel continued to dominate German opera in the early 19th century, although works such as **Faust** (1816) by Spohr reflect contemporary operatic trends by grouping individual numbers into extended scenes and by using short musical ideas, now often called 'reminiscence motifs', to identify characters or events.

The beginning of German Romantic opera occurred in 1821, with the premiere of **Der Freischütz** (The Free-Shooter) by Carl Maria von Weber (1786–1826). Weber was a cousin of Mozart's wife and he was born into a family that ran a company presenting *Singspiel* around rural Germany.

Der Freischütz reflects the *Singspiel* tradition of spoken dialogue between musical numbers, many of which have simple folk-like melodies. However, the work took on a special importance for German identity because it is based on a German legend and all of its principal characters are ordinary German people – foresters and peasants – rather than ancient rulers from faraway lands. All of which led to this type of work becoming known as *romantische Oper* (Romantic opera) – a particularly Germanic type of work for an age when opera was dominated by Italy.

Equally Romantic was Weber's chilling portrayal of the supernatural in the work. The story concerns a young forester, Max, who needs to win a shooting contest if he is to gain the hand of Agatha and succeed her father as head forester. The evil Caspar, whose aim seems perfect, invites Max to the Wolf's Glen at midnight, where he will cast seven magic bullets that are guaranteed to hit their targets.

Caspar arrives first and, as an offstage chorus of invisible spirits moans incantations and a distant bell strikes twelve o'clock, he makes a circle of stones around a skull. Taking out his hunting knife, he plunges it into the skull and calls out 'Samiel! Samiel! Appear!' The devil, masquerading as the huntsman Samiel, appears from a trap door, surrounded by blue light. The audience learns that Caspar has sold his soul and tomorrow is pay day. Caspar makes a bargain with Samiel for three more years on earth in return for the soul of Max, who wants seven magic bullets. Samiel warns that the first six will hit their target, but he will always control the seventh. Before Samiel disappears, he warns that he will be waiting at the gates of hell for either Max or Caspar.

Max arrives and, as Caspar starts to cast the bullets, clouds block out the moon and a crucible of hot metal emits a greenish-white glow. An owl's eyes can be seen in the dark, a black boar bursts through the bushes, a storm starts to brew. Caspar calls out the number of each bullet he makes, and a ghostly echo repeats that number from offstage.

Unseen horses and dogs are heard and fiery wheels emitting sparks spin across the stage. Misty images of hunters and stags fly through the sky, accompanied by offstage voices. Thunder and lightning are followed by torrential rain. Dark blue flames spring from the ground, will-o-the-wisps are seen in the mountains, trees crack and the earth seems to quake. As the seventh bullet is cast, Caspar starts shuddering, and cries out 'Samiel! – Samiel! – Samiel! Help!' A rotten tree is transformed into the devil. Caspar and Max faint as the curtain falls on one of the most extraordinary **coups de théâtre** in opera.

By the climax of the shooting competition, six of the bullets have been successfully used and the final task is to shoot a white dove. Agatha has experienced a number of ill omens and, as Max takes aim, she cries out not to shoot. As he fires, she faints and Caspar is struck by the seventh bullet. Samiel rises from the earth to claim Caspar, who collapses, cursing both heaven and hell. The opera ends with rejoicing for the forthcoming marriage of Max and Agatha.

The Wolf's Glen scene is justly famous as an example of the descriptive power of the Romantic style in music. Much of it is set to melodrama, with both Samiel (a non-singing part) and Caspar speaking over spine-chilling music based on unsettling chromatic chords. Weber's particularly sensitive ear for orchestral colour includes the oily sound of clarinets in their lowest register, soft trombone chords, offbeat timpani strokes and the constant, quiet agitation of strings playing tremolando.

It is not just the Wolf's Glen scene that made *Der Freischütz* so famous. Weber made unprecedented use of an ensemble of four horns in close harmony to convey a romantic sense of hunting horns echoing through an ancient German woodland, and his treatment of the start of the final act was particularly admired. In contrast to the stormy horrors of the Wolf's Glen, it is set in Agatha's bedroom the next morning. She is dressed in bridal white and a vase of white roses is lit by a shaft of sunlight coming through the windows as she sings of the sun's warm rays. The entire scenario was praised for its union of poetry, music, scenery and lighting – a feature of opera that was to become particularly important in the work of Wagner, later in the century.

The overture to *Der Freischütz* is also famed for the way in which Weber uses the traditional, abstract structure of sonata form to provide a musical microcosm of the drama that is to follow.

In the slow introduction, a picture of forest life painted by the four horns is suddenly interrupted by an ominous foreshadowing of the supernatural. In the main part of the overture, the agitated theme of Max's first aria leads, via a reference to the Wolf's Glen music, to the optimism of Agatha's aria in Act Two, eventually culminating in a change from the darkness of C minor to the glorious light of C major, anticipating the triumph of love over evil with which the opera will end.

Weber was to write two more *romantische Opern*, **Euryanthe** (1823) and **Oberon** (1826). Neither achieved the popularity of *Der Freischütz* and are rarely performed today. *Euryanthe* is notable for being **through-composed** – the work is set to music throughout, with no sections of spoken dialogue, and there is no clear distinction between recitatives and arias. Once again, this is something that would influence the work of Wagner.

Although Weber established a distinctly German type of opera with *Der Freischütz*, its popularity was also due to the fascination of the age with the supernatural. Mary Shelley's novel *Frankenstein* was published in 1818, just three years before the first performance of *Der Freischütz*, and magic lanterns that projected scary images of skeletons, demons and ghosts were particularly popular at this time. Indeed the various images that raise the goose-bumps in the Wolf Glen's scene of *Der Freischütz* parallel this love of phantasmagoria.

Heinrich Marschner (1795–1861) had considerable success with his *romantische Opern*, **Der Vampyr** (1828) and **Hans Heiling** (1833), which make use of supernatural effects, although both works have now fallen out of fashion. The supernatural also plays a major part in Wagner's first major success, discussed below.

Some of the best-known German and Austrian composers, including Schubert, Mendelssohn and Schumann, had little success with opera, and neither Brahms nor Bruckner wrote for the stage. However, one composer came to dominate German opera in the second half of the 19th century.

Richard Wagner (1813–1883) was no child prodigy. As a schoolboy he was more interested in literature than music, and he had ambitions to become a playwright. However, he became increasingly interested in music, took lessons and worked in various provincial opera houses, conducting Marschner's *Der Vampyr* in 1833. Wagner's first two attempts at writing an opera were not a success and eventually he and his wife went on the run to avoid their mounting debts. They took a stormy sea trip from Riga (now in Latvia) to London and then settled in Paris from 1839 to 1842.

Wagner found it a struggle to make a living in Paris, and his third opera, *Rienzi,* was turned down by the Paris Opéra, despite being a grand opera in the Meyerbeer tradition, complete with a ballet in the second act. However, with the strong support

The Flying Dutchman staged in Seville

of Meyerbeer, *Rienzi* was performed to great acclaim in Dresden in 1842, and the Wagners settled in the city, delighted to be back on German soil at last.

While in Paris, Wagner had also been working on **Der fliegende Holländer** (The Flying Dutchman) a *romantische Oper* that is rooted in the supernatural tradition and which is the first of his operas to remain in the international repertoire.

It is one of the shortest of Wagner's operas, despite being over two hours in length, and the composer had originally written it as a single act, which he had hoped to persuade the Paris Opéra to stage before a ballet. They purchased Wagner's sketch of the work, but decided against it. It subsequently became the second of Wagner's operas to be premiered in Dresden, in 1843, for which Wagner recast the work in three acts. Because this results in an awkward pattern of two short acts sandwiching a much longer second act, modern productions often revert to Wagner's original intention of presenting the entire opera as a single act, without intervals.

As in all of his mature operas, Wagner wrote his own text, beginning with a prose draft which he then turned into the finished libretto

Wagner's mature operas

Der fliegende Holländer, 1843
Tannhäuser, 1845
Lohengrin, 1850
Tristan und Isolde, 1855
Die Meistersinger von Nürnberg, 1868
Der Ring des Nibelungen, 1876
    (cycle of four operas:
    Das Rheingold, *Die Walküre*,
    Siegfried and *Götterdämmerung*)
Parsifal, 1882

121

(which he preferred to call the the *dichtung* or poem). He claimed that the idea for *The Flying Dutchman* arose from his sea passage from Riga, which had taken three weeks and had involved sheltering from storms in the fjords of Norway. More immediately, though, the plot is loosely based on a story by the German poet, Heinrich Heine, published in 1834, which in turn draws on a nautical legend of a ghost ship doomed forever to sail the oceans. Added to this is the subtext which Wagner would use in many of his later operas: that sin and suffering can be redeemed through a love that is proved by death.

The overture begins with four horns and two bassoons announcing the famous strident 'storm motif' that will recur throughout the opera:

Captain Daland has been forced to find shelter for his ship from a fearsome storm. Suddenly a phantom vessel with blood-red sails crashes alongside. Its Dutch captain has been condemned to roam the seas, only allowed ashore once every seven years.

Wagner's *Der fliegende Holländer*, storm motif

He can only be released from the curse if he can find a wife who will be true to him. He offers Daland treasure in return for marriage to Senta, Daland's daughter.

Back at Daland's house, the women are spinning while they wait for their menfolk to return from the sea. Senta knows the legend of the Dutchman. She has his portrait and dreams of being the woman who will save him. Her suitor, Erik, is convinced that she is possessed by the devil. When Senta's father arrives with the Dutchman, she swears to be true to him until death.

At the harbour that evening, the sailors and their girls sing and dance to celebrate the safe return of Daland's ship. They call out for the crew of The Flying Dutchman to join them – the dance suddenly stops and a strange, distant chord is heard – but there is no reply from the Dutchman. Suddenly the sea starts to rise up around the ghostly Dutch ship, which is lit by a strange blue light. A violent wind whistles through its rigging, which Wagner illustrates by writing chords for three piccolos (with more backstage, if possible), and adding parts for a wind machine and a large tam-tam (gong). The crew of The Flying Dutchman taunt the Norwegian sailors, who run off in fear.

Senta arrives with Erik who reminds her that she had vowed to remain true to him. When the Dutchman sees her with another man and hears this, he thinks he is lost and orders his crew to set sail. As they depart, Senta runs to a cliff top, vowing to be faithful to the Dutchman even in death, and throws herself into the sea. The Flying Dutchman immediately sinks, the sea rises up, and in the distance Senta and the Dutchman are seen in a close embrace, soaring upwards towards the rising sun.

Such a finale is not only very difficult to stage, but clearly indicates that the spirit of grand opera was still very much alive in Wagner's early works. This is also true of his next opera, *Tannhäuser* (1845), which requires some 50 instrumentalists on stage in addition to the orchestra in the pit. Based on a combination of mythology and 14th-century history, the opera is about a struggle between sacred and profane love. The former is symbolised by grand music for processions of knights and pilgrims, and the latter by the sensuality of Wagner's music for the delights of Venus.

Wagner had hoped that *Tannhäuser* would finally establish his reputation in Paris, which was still the centre of the operatic world. Emperor Napoleon III had requested a production of the work in 1861 and, as this would be given by the Paris Opéra, Wagner added the obligatory ballet sequence. For this he developed the original seductive 'Venusberg' music into a *Bacchanale*, in which the increasing chromaticism of Wagner's style across the intervening 15 years is particularly apparent.

The failure of the Paris version became one of the great operatic scandals of the 19th century. To make better dramatic sense of the ballet, Wagner had placed it in Act One rather than in its traditional place in Act Two, with the result that those who came only for the ballet completely missed it. They vented their anger by hissing and whistling while the opera continued. Their fury was particularly directed at Wagner and his Austrian friend, Princess von Metternich, who had helped arrange the production, neither of whom were greatly liked in Paris. On the third night there were several interruptions of up to 15 minutes, after which Wagner cancelled the remaining performances.

One of the highlights of *Tannhäuser* is a singing competition in which a song about the virtue of chastity from a knight named Wolfram von Eschenbach is countered by a lusty air from Tannhäuser in praise of erotic sensuality. Wolfram is believed to have been a real figure from history, a 13th-century poet whose medieval romance called *Parzival* would be the inspiration for Wagner's last opera.

The third in the trilogy of Wagner's middle-period operas is **Lohengrin** (1850), who was the son of Parzival in Wolfram von Eschenbach's account of knightly deeds. Wagner also draws on other sources for his libretto, but the essence of the story is that Lohengrin mysteriously appears in a boat pulled by a swan to save Elsa, who has been falsely accused of murder, by marrying her, on condition that she never asks his name or calling.

For the arrival of the newly wed couple, Wagner composed the wedding march that is now known in English as 'Here comes the bride'. In the opera it tends to sound much grander than is sometimes heard when played on the organ. A great procession of knights and their ladies is accompanied by the full orchestra, plus 15 instruments that start backstage and gradually get nearer as the procession moves closer. Once alone with Lohengrin, Elsa can no longer contain her curiosity and asks the forbidden questions. Lohengrin slays her false accusers, but announces that now his identity is known he must leave her for ever. Elsa dies in her brother's arms.

Wagner had completed *Lohengrin* by 1849, when he found himself on the wrong side of an uprising in Dresden calling for constitutional reform and the unification of Germany. Following the issue of an arrest warrant, Wagner went on the run once again, eventually settling in Switzerland for the next 12 years. The first performance of *Lohengrin* was eventually given in Weimar, where it was conducted by Wagner's friend, the composer Franz Liszt.

In 1849 Wagner published two essays, followed in 1851 by a full-length book, in which he expounded his view that opera – particularly Italian opera – had been corrupted by superficial plots and virtuoso singing. Music had become an end in its own right, while drama had been neglected. He argued for a new concept of opera, which became known as 'music drama' (although this was not a term that Wagner himself used). He saw this as a union of music, poetry, drama, visual art and stagecraft and he described this as **Gesamtkunstwerk** (union of all the arts).

Wagner saw that this fusion was more likely to succeed if it could be accomplished by one person, and so he saw a need to manage his operas much more closely than before. Not only did he write the texts and the music, he directed the production, supervised stage designers and painters, and provided sketches for costumes and props. Ultimately, he realised that he would need his own opera house to achieve his goals. Remarkably, he was eventually able to realise even that dream.

In the meantime, Wagner began work on the most extraordinarily epic project in the entire history of opera. In the autumn of 1848 he had started drafting the poem for an opera about Siegfried the Dragon-slayer, a folk hero in the mythology of both Iceland and Germany. In pursuit of the art-work of the future, Wagner decided to link this personal saga to the much larger and more universal theme of how the gods of Old Norse mythology brought about their own destruction.

Wagner's genius in doing this was to create a work of universal application that is as relevant today as when it was written, because it deals with how the world is driven by a determination to pursue illusory goals, such as the thirst for power, which ultimately bring suffering rather than happiness. This philosophy is based on the somewhat pessimistic writings of the German philosopher Schopenhauer which Wagner studied closely while working on this project.

Wagner found that the back story to Siegfried needed too much explanation for a single opera. In fact, the complex succession of events eventually required a cycle of four operas (which Wagner preferred to describe as three operas with a preliminary evening), known as **Der Ring des Nibelungen** (The Ring of the Nibelung or The Ring cycle). It took 26 years to complete and the cycle was first performed in 1876 to celebrate the opening of the Bayreuth Festspielhaus (see the box below). The entire Ring cycle takes at least 15 hours to perform, excluding intervals. Each of the operas is sometimes presented separately, often prior to a production of the complete cycle, which is generally presented over the span of a week, rather than on consecutive nights, because some soloists have to sing in as many as three of the operas.

Bayreuth

It is very unlikely that The Ring would ever have been staged or even completed without the enthusiasm of King Ludwig II of Bavaria, who had been crowned in 1864, at the age of 18. He paid off Wagner's considerable debts, funded the completion of The Ring, and eventually paid much of the cost of a brand new opera house for the sole performance of Wagner's operas in the town of Bayreuth. Known as the Bayreuth Festspielhaus (Bayreuth Festival Theatre) it continues to present the composer's operas in a five-week summer festival, and is still directed by members of the Wagner family. Going to Bayreuth is a pilgrimage for many of Wagner's fans and the waiting list for tickets is up to ten years.

Guide to
Wagner's Bayreuth
Festspielhaus

The opera house was designed to Wagner's specifications, and is famed for its warm acoustic, attributed to its mainly wooden interior, its very deep and almost totally hidden orchestra pit, and its excellent lines of sight – the entire audience of nearly 2000 are seated in the fairly steeply raked stalls, with no galleries or boxes.

A necessarily brief outline of the plot is shown in the box overleaf. The story centres on a magic ring that gives unlimited power to those who wear it. It is forged from gold stolen from the depths of the river Rhine by the dwarf Alberich, who curses the ring when it is seized by Wotan, chief of the ancient Nordic gods. Wotan loses the ring to the giants Fafner and Fasolt, and then schemes for two generations to regain it. Ultimately, the power of the gods is broken, humans learn to take responsibility for their own destinies, and the ring is returned to the Rhine from where it came.

The cycle of four operas forms a journey to enlightenment. The characters in *Das Rheingold*, are entirely mythical beings – gods, demi-gods, dwarves, giants and river-nymphs. Humans appear in *Die Walküre*, but they are at the mercy of the gods and do not survive. In *Siegfried*, people start to assert their own will and defy the gods, while *Götterdämmerung* sees human life break free from the influence of the gods, who ultimately perish.

To portray this vast epic in music, Wagner avoided the customary division of acts into separate numbers or even composite *scenas*, and instead created (as he wrote in 1879) 'a penetrating web of basic themes, which are contrasting and complementing each other, which are formed anew, divided and joined in the same manner as in a symphonic movement'.

These 'basic themes', often of only a few notes, are now called **leitmotifs** (guide motifs, or leading motifs). Different commentators have identified at least 80, and possibly some 200, *leitmotifs* in *The Ring*, although Wagner himself never gave any detailed description of them. They are associated with characters, objects, emotions and important dramatic events. Wagner wrote that 'at their hand we become the constant fellow-knowers of the profoundest secret of the poet's aim'. In other words, by allowing listeners to make their own, possibly subconscious, connections and realisations, the audience becomes part of the drama rather than mere onlookers.

The Ring
Das Rheingold (The Rhine Gold)

The great treasure of gold guarded by the Rhinemaidens is stolen by the dwarf Alberich. He makes a ring from a small part of the horde as he has learned that whoever makes such a ring will have power over all the earth.

Two giants, the brothers Fasolt and Fafner, have built a mighty mountain-top fortress called Valhalla for Wotan, king of the gods. They order Wotan to recover the gold from Alberich's subterranean caverns as payment for their work. When Wotan seizes the ring that the dwarf has made, Alberich curses it, warning that it will bring death. Fasolt then grabs the ring and is immediately clubbed to death by his brother, Fafner, who makes off with it.

Following a great storm, a rainbow forms a bridge, across which the gods process into their new home of Valhalla.

Die Walküre (The Valkyrie)

Wotan's son, Siegmund, discovers his twin sister, Sieglinde, from whom he was separated at birth. Despite the fact that she is already married to Siegmund's enemy, Hunding, they fall in love and Siegmund claims her as his wife.

Wotan has also sired nine female warriors, the Valkyries. Their duty is to greet and defend heroes in battle, and to fly them through the air on horseback to Valhalla when they die. Wotan had planned that Siegmund would retrieve the ring from Fafner, but he realises that he cannot defend Siegmund's incestuous relationship and orders his favourite Valkyrie daughter, Brünnhilde, to ensure that Siegmund dies at the hands of Hunding.

Brunnhilde disobeys her father and so Wotan intervenes by shattering the magic sword he had made for Siegmund, freeing the way for Hunding to kill him. Wotan then fells Hunding with a contemptuous wave of his hand.

Brünnhilde retrieves the pieces of the broken sword and entrusts them to the pregnant Sieglinde, but Wotan reduces Brünnhilde to mortal status for her disobedience and sends her to eternal sleep from which she can only be woken by the man who will become her husband. He will be a great hero who has the power to break through the magic fire with which Wotan then surrounds his daughter. That man will be his grandson, Siegfried.

Wagner's *Die Walküre*, Magic Fire Music

Siegfried

Siegfried is the son of Siegmund and Sieglinde. He reforges his father's sword and wins the ring by killing Fafner. He finds Brünnhilde but Wotan tries to stop him wakening her. Siegfried smashes Wotan's spear with the very sword that Wotan had once given his father. Wotan, knowing that his days are ended, vanishes.

Siegfried passes through the wall of fire and kisses Brünnhilde, the first woman he has ever seen. She awakes from her endless sleep and they fall in love, welcoming the fact that they are mortal and will one day die. They bid goodbye to Valhalla and the old order of the gods.

Götterdämmerung (The Twilight of the Gods)

The three Norns, who spin the fate of the world, tell the story of Wotan's ruin and how he will bring about the destruction of Valhalla. They can see no clear future beyond that and their thread of fate breaks in their hands.

In a palace on the Rhine, the villainous Hagen, son of Alberich, drugs Siegfried, who has given the ring to Brünnhilde, and tricks him into retrieving the ring and betraying her. She, in turn, reveals that the only way to kill Siegfried is to stab him in the back. Hagen kills Siegfried and then slays his own half brother in a quarrel over the ring. As he tries to remove it from Siegfried's finger, the dead arm rises to threaten him.

Brünnhilde orders a great funeral pyre to be lit. She takes the ring from Siegfried's finger before his body is set alight, and then rides her horse into the flames to join Siegfried in death and redeem the world. As she does so, the Rhine overflows its banks, the Rhinemaidens rise up and seize the ring. Hagen drowns in the depths of the river, where his father Alberich had begun the entire tragedy, and Valhalla and the gods are burned to the ground.

For example, the 'Ring motif' (marked *a* opposite) is first heard in *Das Rheingold* when Alberich is told by one of the Rhinemaidens that a ring made from their gold could give the wearer unlimited power. Alberich's eyes are transfixed by the gold as he sings variant *b* of the motif. In a transition from night to dawn, that goes from the bottom of the Rhine to mountain tops covered in mist and cloud, the motif starts to transform (*c*). Then, as day breaks and a magnificent new castle high above the Rhine swings into view, the 'Ring motif' has metamorphosed into the 'Valhalla motif' (*d*). The symbol of Alberich's power has become the symbol of Wotan's power, and subconsciously the audience already seems to know that Wotan's new fortress will be paid for with Alberich's stolen gold.

Wotan surrounds Brünnhilde with fire at the end of *Die Walküre* (San Francisco Opera)

Eventually the Valhalla motif becomes associated with Wotan himself, and is heard at times when he is spoken of, or remembered in his absence.

Sometimes the meaning of a motif is not immediately clear. Near the end of *Das Rheingold* Wotan is seized by an idea to save the future of his race. He tells nobody what it is, but the orchestra plays an upward-thrusting theme that is only discovered in the next opera to be the 'sword motif' – the all-powerful sword that will not, as it turns out, manage to save Wotan's son, and that will eventually be used against Wotan by his own grandson:

Throughout *The Ring* Wagner spins a web of *leitmotifs* that are constantly re-arranged and developed to underpin the dramatic scenario of the work. They form a continuity that became known as *unendliche Melodie* – literally, endless melody, but meaning in practice that every melodic note has thematic importance.

As befits a work of epic proportions, *The Ring* requires a huge orchestra. On average for each opera Wagner requires 16 woodwind, 18 brass, 64 strings, 6 harps, timpani and an array of percussion – totalling more than 100 musicians in the pit orchestra. In addition, the large number of offstage sound effects includes 18 anvils, a thunder machine, more harps and three alpenhorns. Today, some compromises usually have to be made to this specification, even in the largest opera houses!

The very large brass section resulted from Wagner increasing the size of the horn section from the then standard four to eight players, adding a bass trumpet to a section of three standard trumpets, and adding both a bass and a contrabass trombone to a section of three tenor trombones.

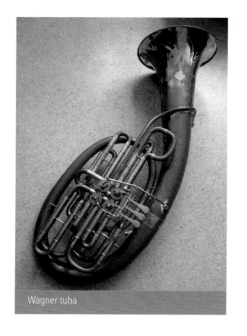
Wagner tuba

In addition, Wagner had four special brass instruments built to his specifications. Known as **Wagner tubas**, they are played by four of the hornists where their weighty, yet gentle tone is required.

Despite its enormous size, the orchestra for *The Ring* was prevented from overbalancing the singers by Wagner's design for the orchestra pit at Bayreuth. The front part has an acoustic cover above the players and the rear is deep below the stage. Only the quieter instruments are placed in the central uncovered portion, where they can speak directly into the auditorium.

By 1857 Wagner had completed all of the text of *The Ring*, as well as the music for the first two operas in the cycle, and was making good progress on *Siegfried*, when he suddenly stopped work on the project. Perhaps this was because of the seeming impossibility of getting the work performed, or possibly it was due to a crisis in the composer's life triggered by an extra-marital affair he was having. Whatever the cause, his thoughts were turning towards a new opera – a work that could be completed within a more realistic time span than *The Ring*.

That opera was ***Tristan und Isolde*** (Tristan and Isolda), which Wagner finished in August 1859. The work proved too difficult to stage in Vienna, and eventually it was first performed in Munich in 1865. Its mystical libretto is based on a medieval romance, dating back at least to the 12th century, which tells of the passionate but doomed love of Tristan, a knight from Cornwall, and Isolde, a princess from Ireland.

Wagner kept the action to a minimum, and much of the work is concerned with the thoughts and feelings of its two protagonists, who eventually resolve to die in order that their identities can merge as one. The opera reflects Wagner's study of Buddhist literature, with its message that desire causes pain and can only be overcome with wisdom. It also reflects his study of Schopenhauer's writings about sexual desire and death, particularly evident in Isolde's final *liebestod* (love death), sung over Tristan's corpse, at the end of which she herself dies.

Throughout the opera, Wagner expresses the endless yearning of the lovers through restless chromatic writing that rarely seems to find resolution. The style was far in advance of its day, and was to influence several generations of later composers. Indeed, some saw *Tristan und Isolde* as the beginning of the end for conventional harmony and for the system of major and minor keys used in music since the beginning of opera. It was laying some of the foundations for 20th-century modernism.

Wagner's fortunes were at their lowest in the early 1860s, with the fiasco of the Paris *Tannhäuser* in 1861, the difficulty in bringing both The Ring and *Tristan und Isolde* to the stage and, in 1862, separation from his first wife. Despite so many problems, in late 1861 Wagner started work in earnest on a project that he had first began to sketch out in 1845.

featured opera

Die Meistersinger von Nürnberg (The Mastersingers of Nuremberg) is the only comedy among Wagner's mature operas, although it would be more accurate to describe it as a genial romance than any sort of side-splitting farce. The opera contains no supernatural events or historical myths, and is based on an entirely original story by Wagner, although some of the characters are real figures from history.

As if to underline its uniqueness, Wagner brings back a number of the operatic conventions that he had previously rejected. So, the libretto is entirely in rhymed verse, and the work is essentially a number opera, with a string of arias, serenades, duets, choruses, a quintet and ensemble finales. However, there is no recitative and Wagner weaves a characteristic network of *leitmotifs* through the work.

The Mastersingers could hardly be more different from the relentless chromaticism of *Tristan und Isolde* – indeed Wagner even included a suitably yearning quotation from the latter in *The Mastersingers*, followed by a joke about the irresponsible Tristan.

The opera takes place in Nuremberg, Bavaria in about 1560, and centres on the real-life guild of *Meistersinger* (Mastersingers), who were an association of amateur poets and musicians, and mostly skilled craftsmen by trade. They aimed to maintain high standards in the art of formal singing through a complex system of rules, as well as by training apprentices and running song contests. The principal characters in the opera are:

Hans Sachs, cobbler and Mastersinger

Veit Pogner, goldsmith and Mastersinger

Sixtus Beckmesser, town clerk and Mastersinger

Fritz Kothner, baker and Mastersinger

David, apprentice to Sachs

Eva, Pogner's daughter

Magdalena, Eva's companion

Walther von Stolzing, knight

Eight other Mastersingers, Nightwatchman, Chorus of guild members and their wives, journeymen, apprentices, young women and people of Nuremberg

Hans Sachs was an actual historical figure, and the pedantic Beckmesser may have been based on Eduard Hanslick, a music critic who increasingly spoke out against Wagner's music, although it is more likely that Beckmesser is simply a caricature of critics in general.

In 1862 Wagner completed and conducted the overture (which he described as a *Vorspiel* or Prelude) before starting to compose the music for the opera itself in the spring of 1863. Nevertheless, he must have had a clear idea from the outset of how he intended to proceed, as some 13 *leitmotifs* from the opera are introduced in the overture, starting with five of its main themes.

The first is the noble theme of the Mastersingers Guild (motif *a* in the next example), followed by a motif associated with Walther's love for Eva. Wagner then introduces a martial theme (*b*), developed from what is thought to be an actual Mastersinger melody published in 1697. This is followed by the motif of the artistic brotherhood of the guild, developed from the same 1697 source, and rounded off by a theme (*c*) that will form the melody of the prize-winning song at the climax of the opera.

These themes, along with other motifs from the opera, are developed in the central part of the overture before Wagner brings back *a*, *b* and *c* simultaneously, in a feat of brilliant contrapuntal dexterity:

The overture leads, without a break, into Act One, with the curtain rising on the interior of a church where the congregation are singing the final chorale (hymn) of a service. Between the phrases, Walther is trying to catch the eye of Eva Pogner.

After the parishioners have left, he learns that she is to be married the next day to the winner of a singing competition organised by the Mastersingers. Walther decides to enter the contest and David (the sweetheart of Eva's companion Magdalena) is asked to explain the complicated rules, as he is an apprentice Mastersinger.

Twelve Mastersingers enter the church for a committee meeting. The wealthy Pogner confirms that in the interests of art he will offer all his possessions as well as the hand of his daughter to whoever wins the song competition. Sachs thinks that Eva should have a say in the matter, but his objection is voted down, while the wily old Beckmesser thinks he is in with a chance.

Walther introduces himself as a self-taught singer-songwriter, and is allowed to perform a test song. Beckmesser enters the marker's box and, every time he hears a violation of the rules, he sighs and groans, and noisily scratches down details of the fault on his slate. After seven errors Walther fails his audition and stalks out, leaving the Mastersingers squabbling and their apprentices dancing in circles around them. After all have left, Sachs reflects on the natural beauty of Walther's song.

Act Two takes place a few hours later, during a warm midsummer evening on the medieval streets of Nuremberg. Walther proposes eloping with Eva, but they have to hide when the nightwatchman passes. Suddenly Beckmesser arrives to serenade Eva. She persuades Magdalena to impersonate her, while she and Walther watch. No sooner does the elderly town clerk finish tuning his lute, than loud singing and hammering comes from the nearby cobblers' shop. Hans Sachs says he is repairing the shoes that Beckmesser urgently needs for the song contest next day.

Sachs ends up acting as marker for Beckmesser's truly awful serenade by knocking a nail into the shoes each time the town clerk breaks a rule of style in his song. As Beckmesser's singing gets worse and worse, Sachs bangs away with increasing fury until David is woken by the noise. He sees Beckmesser apparently serenading his sweetheart, Magdalena, climbs out of a window and throws himself on the town clerk. The increasing racket wakes the entire city, and all come out in their night clothes, some armed with clubs, to join a free-for-all. At last, the nightwatchman's horn is heard, the women pour pails and jugs of water over the people in the street below, and the riot ends just as quickly as it began.

Act Three begins with Hans Sachs pondering how he can resolve the madness of the world. Walther arrives to tell Sachs of a dream he has had, and the cobbler recognises that it could form the makings of a prize song. He explains the structure of a Mastersong to Walther and writes down the words dictated by the knight.

Walther delivers his Prize Song to the people of Nuremberg (*The Mastersingers* at Glyndebourne Opera House)

After they have left, Beckmesser hobbles into Sachs's shop, still sore from the night before. He finds Walther's poem, but assumes it is by Sachs whom he imagines is entering the competition to win Eva's hand. He is caught red-handed by Sachs, who tells him to keep the poem, but warns that it will be hard to sing.

Eva arrives in her wedding dress and Walther returns to sing the latest version of his song to her. Sachs has always had a soft spot for Eva but, with great resignation, places her in Walther's arms. David and Magdalena arrive, and Sachs promotes his young apprentice to journeyman. All five sing a quintet in praise of the happiness that the new song promises to bring.

The scene changes to a meadow outside the city, the spires of which can be seen in the distance. It is midsummer's day, the feast of St John the Baptist and a holiday. Jugglers, acrobats and other acts are entertaining the people. Onstage trumpets and drums announce a grand procession of guilds, each preceded by their banner, and they are followed by the Mastersingers in their finest robes.

The song contest opens with Beckmesser hopelessly trying to fit Walther's verses to his own melody. He forgets some words, garbles the rest and ends up singing total nonsense. After he has been laughed off the podium, Beckmesser tells the crowds that the awful song was written by their beloved Sachs. The cobbler denies this and says that the song is beautiful when sung properly by its composer. He calls forward Walther, not as a contestant (for he failed to qualify for the contest) but as a witness to the power of the song, which he sings to the murmured approval of the crowd:

Molto moderato

Mor - gen - lich   leuch - tend ___ im ___ ro   -   si - gen Schein, von Blüth' und Duft

Everyone is entranced, and Eva places the laureate's wreath on Walther's head, but the knight initially refuses the Mastersingers' chain of office and medallion. Sachs tells him to honour the guild that has given him Eva, and not to scorn it. In a finale that it is reported Wagner came to regret, Sachs gives a long explanation of how the guild has preserved German art against its enemies.

Wagner's *Die Meistersinger von Nürnberg*, 'Morgenlich leuchtend'

Sachs then presents Walther with the chain of office, Eva replaces the wreath on Sachs's head, and everyone hails Nuremberg's dear Hans Sachs.

Wagner's interest in historicism is clear in much of *The Mastersingers*, particularly in his treatment of the nature of song which, along with bringing order out of chaos, is at the heart of the opera. Sachs explains to Walther the traditional structure of an art song as the real Mastersingers would have known it. Known as *Bar* form, it should have two *Stollen* (stanzas) of equal length, sung to the same melody, followed by an *Abgesang* (conclusion) that should introduce a different but not unrelated idea, and which may equal the combined length of the two *Stollen*. One of the reasons why Sachs so admired Walther's song-writing talent was because the young knight treated the structure innovatively, and was not hide-bound by the rules.

A number of arias in *The Mastersingers* are written in *Bar* form, although Wagner mistakenly thought that the term referred to the structure of a single verse, rather than the whole song. Indeed, the entire opera can be said to resemble a huge *Bar* form in that the first two acts are of similar length, each ending with a riot that leaves a single person on stage, like a pair of *Stollen*, while the final act, at twice the length of either of the first two, provides the conclusion and explanation of the drama.

Die Meistersinger von Nürnberg was first performed to great acclaim in 1868, in Munich, thanks to the patronage of King Ludwig II of Bavaria. Consisting of some five hours of music (without intervals) it is one of the longest works in the standard operatic repertoire. Performances generally start in the afternoon, with a long interval for dinner before Act Three, in order to avoid an unrealistically late finish.

Following the death of his first wife, in 1870 Wagner married Cosima, daughter of the composer Franz Liszt and 24 years his junior. They had previously had an affair while she was still married to the conductor Hans von Bülow. Much of Wagner's time in the 1870s was spent in planning the new opera house at Bayreuth and its opening production of *The Ring* in 1876.

Wagner then began work on his final opera, **Parsifal**, which is loosely based on two medieval sources, *Perceval, le Conte du Graal* (Perceval, the Story of the Grail) written by Chrétien de Troyes in the 1180s, and *Parzival* by Wolfram von Eschenbach, written a few decades later and largely based on the earlier text. It tells a mystical story of how the arrogant knight Parsifal learns wisdom through pity for the suffering of others. Wagner described *Parsifal* as 'a festival play for the consecration of the stage' and it was first performed at the second Bayreuth Festival in 1882.

The death of Wagner in 1883 left a void in the production of new German opera. Engelbert Humperdinck (1854–1921), who had assisted in the premiere of *Parsifal* at Bayreuth, produced an enduring success with **Hänsel und Gretel** (1893), based on the fairy tale of the same name by the Brothers Grimm and which is Wagnerian in its use of *leitmotifs* and in its richly detailed orchestration. However, Wagner's legacy would eventually be inherited by Richard Strauss, who was appointed to the music staff at Bayreuth in 1889 but whose mature operas all date from the 20th century and are therefore outlined in the next chapter.

Nationalism

Until the first quarter of the 19th century, the mainstream tradition in classical music had been dominated by composers from Italy, France, Germany and Austria. The term 'Nationalism' is a handy, if rather imprecise, label for movements that developed in other countries that came to develop artistic traditions of their own. Opera was an important vehicle in asserting nationalism because it could draw on folklore and legends in its stories, and on folk idioms in its music.

In many countries, opera was at first an exotic import, composed by Italians and performed by visiting troupes from Italy. Gradually, native musicians began to copy these works, with later generations using librettos in the vernacular and eventually finding their own distinctive musical styles.

Russia

Empress Catherine II (Catherine the Great) had ample resources to tempt Italian composers to work at her court in St Petersburg and to send Russian composers to study in Italy during the second half of the 18th century.

Even as late as 1830, Mikhail Glinka (1804–1857) spent three years furthering his musical studies in Italy, with the result that the influence of the *bel canto* style of Bellini and Donizetti can be heard in his first opera, *A Life for the Tsar.* Although earlier Russian composers had written *Singspiel* that were arguably more Russian in style, Glinka's opera was seen as a more cosmopolitan work – an ambassador for Russian music and thus deserving of being described as the first Russian opera. It was first performed at the Bolshoi Theatre in St Petersburg in 1836, and tells the story of a hero of the 17th century who gave his life for the Russian Tsar. Glinka integrated a certain amount of folk music into the opera, but much of its contemporary significance was due to the way it linked the Russian nation with the dynastic authority of the Tsars.

The second of Glinka's two operas was **Ruslan and Lyudmila** (1842), which is based on a poem by Alexander Pushkin. Ruslan is a knight who attempts to rescue Lyudmila, the daughter of the Prince of Kiev abducted by an evil wizard. Both operas are now remembered in the west mainly for their overtures, which are popular short concert works.

Of the various operas planned and begun by Modest Mussorgsky (1839–1881), the only one to be completed was **Boris Godunov**. The original version was based on a play by Pushkin, with a libretto by the composer, which tells the story of the troubled Tsar Boris of Russia who ruled from 1598 to 1605. After this version was turned down by the Imperial Theatres, Mussorgsky substantially rewrote the opera for performance at the Mariinsky Theatre in St Petersburg in 1874.

Boris Godunov is essentially grand opera, from the magnificent coronation scene in its extensive prologue onwards. The most famous opera by Pyotr Tchaikovsky (1840–1893), **Eugene Onegin** (1879), is also based on a work by Pushkin, but on a much more intimate scale. Indeed, the first performance was given by students of the Moscow Imperial Conservatory in the relatively small Maly Theatre.

The original unhappy love story was well known in Russia, and so Tchaikovsky treated it in episodic fashion, as a series of highlights, and with a good deal more sympathy than Pushkin in his original verse novel. Lensky introduces Tatiana, his fiancée's sister, to his friend Onegin. She is smitten, but he is not. Later, Onegin flirts with Lensky's fiancée, resulting in a duel in which he kills Lensky. Some years later Onegin, who has never found happiness, meets Tatiana again. She admits she still loves him, but will never leave her husband.

Tchaikovsky wrote 10 operas, but the only other one to be performed outside Russia with any regularity is **The Queen of Spades** (1890). Once again, the libretto is based on a short story by Pushkin, centred on an officer destroyed by a gambling addiction.

The year 1890 also saw the first performance of the opera **Prince Igor**. Begun in 1868 by Aleksandr Borodin (1833–1887), it remained unfinished at the composer's death and was completed by fellow composers Rimsky-Korsakov and Glazunov. The thrilling choral dances from Act Two, known as the *Polovtsian Dances*, are much more likely to be heard in the concert hall than in the theatre, as the complete opera is rarely staged today in the west.

For a long time, the operas of Nikolai Rimsky-Korsakov (1844–1908) were also known in the west mainly through concert-hall excerpts, such as 'The Flight of the Bumble Bee' from **Tsar Saltan** (1900), based on a fairy-tale poem by Pushkin. One exception has been his final opera, **Le coq d'or** (The Golden Cockerel, 1909, also based on Pushkin), but some of Rimsky-Korsakov's earlier works are now being rediscovered, including the epic **Sadko** (1898) and **The Legend of the Invisible City of Kitezh** (1907).

Bohemia

Bohemia was a region in central Europe that in the 19th century formed part of the Austrian (later the Austro-Hungarian) Empire. Much of Bohemia is now within the Czech Republic whose capital city, Prague, was previously capital of Bohemia.

As one of the cultural centres of the empire, Prague had a long tradition of opera before the start of the 19th century. Mozart's *The Marriage of Figaro* was staged there to great acclaim in 1786, only months after its premiere in Vienna, and the first hugely successful run of his *Don Giovanni* took place at the Estates Theatre in Prague the very next year. Furthermore, Mozart's final *opera seria*, *La clemenza di Tito*, was commissioned for performance in Prague to celebrate the coronation of Leopold II as King of Bohemia.

However, such works were essentially foreign imports. Indeed, the Estates Theatre had been founded in 1783 primarily for the performance of Italian opera and German drama in Prague. As Austrian power diminished in the 19th century, so national awareness increased. The Prague Provisional Theatre was opened in 1862 as a temporary home for national drama and opera, although the first opera to be produced there was by Cherubini, as no Bohemian opera was deemed worthy of such an honour.

That was soon remedied by Bedřich Smetana (1824–1884), who became increasingly identified as the father of Czech music. The most popular of his nine operas, **The Bartered Bride**, was first performed at the Provisional Theatre in 1866 as a two-act comic opera, with spoken dialogue. The libretto is by the Czech writer and journalist Karel Sabina. It was not an immediate success and Smetana made several revisions. By 1870 he had turned it into a three-act opera with recitatives.

The opera is set in rural Bohemia and tells the story of two young lovers, Mařenka and Jeník. Mařenka's parents have promised her in marriage to the simpleton Vašek in order to pay off a debt to his father, Micha. Jeník gets the marriage contract worded to read that Mařenka must marry 'a son of Micha', before revealing that he too is a long-lost son of Micha, from an earlier marriage, and can thus marry Mařenka. The arrival of a visiting circus in the village in the last act offers the opportunity to include a Spanish dancer, a tight-rope walker, a sword-swallower and a drunk (eventually replaced by the hapless Vašek) pretending to be a dancing bear. Few producers can resist adding further colourful circus acts to those prescribed in the libretto!

By and large, Smetana avoids any obvious 'folkiness' in the opera, although he does include Bohemian folk-dance styles such as the polka and the furiant. At the time, the work was regarded as a celebration of nationalism more because of its use of the Czech language and its setting in rural Bohemia. Today *The Bartered Bride* is often performed in German or English, as Czech is not widely spoken, and it has become a great favourite with amateur, as well as professional, opera companies.

The most famous Czech composer in the late-Romantic period was Antonín Dvořák (1841–1904). Of his ten operas, the one most commonly performed in the west is **Rusalka** (1900). Like Humperdinck's *Hänsel and Gretel* of 1893, it is an example of *Märchenoper* – the slightly scary type of fairy-tale opera that briefly became popular in the final years of the 19th century. The opera tells the story of a rusalka (water-nymph) whose love for a human prince has disastrous consequences. Rusalka's Act One aria, 'Song to the Moon' is a frequently performed excerpt from the opera.

Operetta

As opera in the 19th century got longer and grander, a new middle-class audience developed a taste for works that were shorter and more varied. Memorable tunes and colourful orchestration were important, as were amusing (if implausible) plots, action sped along by spoken dialogue between the songs, perhaps a little dancing and, above all, a libretto written in the local language so that the jokes could be understood. The result was operetta (Italian for 'little opera'), a genre that developed primarily in the cities of Paris (where it was known as **opéra bouffe**), London and Vienna.

German-born Jacques Offenbach (1819–1880), who became a French citizen, wrote a large number of operettas to words by Ludovic Halévy and others. His first big success came in 1858 with **Orphée aux enfers** (Orpheus in the Underworld) in which the Greek myth is hilariously sent up – almost literally, for the gods ascend to Mount Olympus in a balloon at the end of the first act.

The entire work is essentially a satire on the upper-class taste for opera, particularly Gluck's *Orfeo ed Euridice*. Instead of being the singer of legend, Offenbach's Orpheus is a bad violinist, whose wife cannot stand his playing or his dreary personality. He threatens her with a three-hour solo in their opening duet. One absurdity quickly leads to another as disguises cause mistaken identities and conspiracies go wrong. Along the way, the audience is entertained to storm effects, dances and transformation scenes. Being operetta, all ends happily – in place of the tragic conclusion of the original myth, the gods throw a party and have a wild dance:

Offenbach's *Orphée aux enfers*, 'Ce bal est original'

Offenbach describes this as a 'galop' – a fast ballroom dance that became popular in the 1820s and that was used by Rossini in 1829 for the final section of his *William Tell* overture. However, the audience would have recognised the galop in *Orpheus* as the even faster *cancan* (French for 'scandal') – a saucy dance routine for the stage rather than the ballroom, involving a chorus line of female dancers doing leg splits and high kicks that exposed a good deal of leg.

After the *cancan* Offenbach and Halévy leave no doubt about the target of their satire as Orpheus enters playing the famous melody from Gluck's *Orfeo ed Euridice* quoted on page 55. The very sound of it sends Eurydice running, as she is rather enjoying her new life with Jupiter and Pluto. In the end, she can't decide between either of them and chooses Bacchus instead, which is just the cue for a reprise of the *cancan* (a tone higher than before for extra thrills).

Other common features of operetta found in *Orpheus in the Underworld* include songs in waltz rhythm (the most popular of all 19th-century dances) and a potpourri overture to whet the audience's appetite with tunes from the show. In operetta, such overtures were frequently assembled at the last minute, often by the composer's assistant. The one now commonly associated with *Orpheus in the Underworld* was written by the Austrian Carl Binder for the opera's 1860 premiere in Vienna.

After *Orpheus*, Offenbach consolidated his reputation with a string of popular operettas that include:

- *La belle Hélène* (The Beautiful Helen, 1864) – another satire on the ancient world.

- *La vie parisienne* (Parisian Life, 1866) – a much more modern story that opens in a railway station with the staff singing out the names of all the wonderful places in France that can be reached by train.

- *La Grande-Duchesse de Gérolstein* (1867) – a political satire that centres on the havoc wreaked by the female ruler of a tiny and imaginary European state, who has a weakness for young men in uniform.

The success of *La Grande-Duchesse de Gérolstein* in London, where it was staged only seven months after its Paris premiere, generated a demand for native works of similar quality that would reflect a more English style of humour, and avoid some of the more risqué elements of French operetta.

This demand was satisfied by the impresario Richard D'Oyly Carte, who wanted a short work to share the bill with Offenbach's **La Périchole**. He commissioned the comedy writer W. S. Gilbert and the young composer Arthur Sullivan to create a one-act operetta. The result was **Trial by Jury** (1875) and its success launched Gilbert and Sullivan on a succession of works known as the Savoy operas, named after the Savoy Theatre that D'Oyly Carte later built for their production.

Gilbert and Sullivan wrote 12 more operettas together, including **HMS Pinafore** (1878), **The Pirates of Penzance** (1879), **The Mikado** (1885), **The Yeomen of the Guard** (1888) and **The Gondoliers** (1889). Amusingly reflecting what it is to be English, these works have proved to be continually popular throughout the English-speaking world. The D'Oyly Carte Opera Company staged professional productions of Gilbert and Sullivan throughout the year for more than a century, and the works form the core repertory of many amateur operatic groups. Operetta, including works by Gilbert and Sullivan, is also sometimes produced by companies such as English National Opera, Opera North, New York City Opera and Lyric Opera of Chicago.

The success of 'G&S', as this repertory is affectionately known, was in part due to Gilbert's particularly English sense of humour, which revelled in absurdity. The plot of *The Pirates of Penzance* revolves around a mishearing that resulted in Frederic, the male lead, being apprenticed until his 21st birthday as a pirate instead of a pilot. In a typically Gilbertian twist, he then discovers that he was born on the 29th of February in a leap year – so he will be in his eighties by the time he has had 21 birthdays.

Poking fun at officialdom is another essentially English trait found in the operettas. *Pirates* includes a 'very model of a modern major-general', whose comprehensive grasp of matters intellectual is matched only by his total ignorance of things military. Similarly, *Pinafore* parodies desk-bound officials, with a First Lord of the Admiralty who advises 'Stick close to your desks and never go to sea, And you all may be rulers of the Queen's Navy!'. In *Iolanthe* (1882) the object of Gilbert's satire is no less than the entire House of Lords, who 'did nothing in particular, and did it very well'.

Although Gilbert's love of puns can sometimes seem dated, he could seize on phrases so memorable that they have entered the English language as sayings in their own right – for example, 'a short, sharp shock' and 'let the punishment fit the crime' (both from *The Mikado*), 'a policeman's lot is not a happy one' (*The Pirates of Penzance*) and 'What never? Well, hardly ever!' (*HMS Pinafore*).

Equally important was Sullivan's ability to create sparkling melodies and to write fluently in almost any style. Parody of serious opera was an important element in the work of G&S from the outset. *Trial by Jury* includes a quartet ('A nice dilemma we have here') that mimics the type of elaborate vocal ensemble popular in *bel canto* opera, and a chorus of welcome from the sycophantic jury ('All hail great judge') that sounds as if it had leapt from the pages of an oratorio by Handel.

In **The Sorcerer** (1877), Sullivan's setting of the 'incantation scene' is a parody of Weber's music for the Wolf's Glen in *Der Freischütz* and Sullivan's Act One finale is a pastiche of an Italian operatic **brindisi** or drinking song, except that in *The Sorcerer* the beverage is tea (a little stab at the 19th-century temperance movement).

There are musical echoes of Wagner in **Iolanthe** (1882), and even a four-note *leitmotif* to fit the four syllables of the eponymous fairy's name. However, instead of three Rhinemaidens swimming in the mighty River Rhine, the bedraggled Iolanthe emerges from a small stream, covered in water weeds.

Sullivan's gift for pastiche is evident throughout the Savoy operas. *The Mikado* contains a modern version of a madrigal ('Brightly dawns our wedding day') while *The Gondoliers* includes a vocal ensemble in the style of an ancient gavotte ('I am a courtier grave and serious'), and ends with castanets flying in a magnificent Spanish dance called a *cachucha*.

Jonathan Miller's 1987 production of *The Mikado* for English National Opera was set in a luxury hotel of the 1930s, with decor and costumes almost entirely in black, white and cream

All of the Savoy operas are noted for the variety of their vocal numbers, ranging from quasi-serious solo ballads and soliloquies to lively solos with choral refrains, duets, trios, elaborate ensembles and climactic finales. The chorus plays an important part in all of the works, and is one of the reasons why they have remained so popular with amateur groups.

A particular speciality of G&S, was the patter song, although this too was simply a parody of the rapid type of operatic aria used by Donizetti, Rossini and Mozart, and that can be traced back to Pergolesi's *La Serva Padrona* of 1733. The big difference is that in Gilbert and Sullivan the rapid stream of tongue-twisting words can actually be understood by all of an English-speaking audience, as in this example from **Ruddigore** (1887):

My eyes are ful-ly o-pen to my aw-ful sit-u-a-tion ± I shall go at once to Ro-der-ic and make him an o-ra-tion, I shall tell him I've re-co-vered my for-got-ten mor-al sen-ses,

Patter songs became so associated with the Savoy operas that Gilbert and Sullivan were able to parody themselves in this patter trio, which memorably ends with the line: 'This particularly rapid, unintelligible patter isn't generally heard, and if it is it doesn't matter.'

Gilbert & Sullivan's *Ruddigore*, patter song

Austria's answer to Offenbach was Johann Strauss II, long known as the 'waltz king'. His third operetta, **Die Fledermaus** (The Bat) appeared in 1874. It was initially far from a triumph, perhaps because of its convoluted plot, but Strauss's music ensured that it would quickly become one of the best-loved operettas of the 19th century.

Die Fledermaus contains little of the pithy satire seen in many of the works discussed so far. It is essentially a domestic farce about a wealthy couple who spend much of the operetta deceiving each other about various indiscretions, only to find each other out by the end.

The centrepiece of the work is a grand masked ball – the traditional vehicle for a succession of mistaken identities and resulting mishaps – for which Strauss wrote a succession of opulent dance-based songs, including a Hungarian *czardas* for the wife, who is out to trick her husband into flirting with her in the belief that she is a visiting countess from Hungary. At the ball the hapless husband catches the eye of an 'actress' (it is actually their own maid in disguise), and suggests to her that he feels sure they've met before. Her mocking response is 'Mein Herr Marquis' – popularly known as 'the laughing song' for obvious reasons. As can be seen from this short excerpt, Strauss did on occasion write demanding vocal lines of a type more associated with grand opera than operetta:

Johann Strauss's *Die Fledermaus*, The laughing song

Ja sehr komisch,   ha   ha   ha,   ist die Sa - che,   ha   ha   ha,   drum verzeihn Sie,   ha   ha   ha,

Strauss's famous polka, *Unter Donner und Blitz* (Thunder and Lightening) is often included in the sequence of dances at the masked ball, which ends with one of the composer's best-loved waltzes:

Johann Strauss's *Die Fledermaus*, waltz

Ha, welch ein Fest, wel - che Nacht voll Freud!   Lie - be und Wein giebt uns Se - lig - keit;

Johann Strauss II continued writing operettas until his death in 1899, achieving another great success with **Der Zigeunerbaron** (The Gypsy Baron) in 1885. The Viennese style of operetta continued into the 20th century with Franz Lehár. His best-known work is **Die lustige Witwe** (The Merry Widow) of 1905, a tuneful and amusing account of a wealthy widow's attempts to find a new husband.

Lehár's operettas had a direct influence on the romantic musical comedies of the early 20th century. Indeed, if you listen to Lehár's dreamy hit song 'Dein ist mein ganzes Herz' (You are my heart's delight), you might well think it was from a musical rather than from his 1929 operetta **Das Land des Lächelns** (The Land of Smiles):

Lehár's *Das Land des Lächelns*, 'Dein ist mein ganzes Herz!'

1929 was also the year in which **The Desert Song**, an American operetta from 1926 by Hungarian-born Sigmund Romberg, was turned into the world's first major film musical. The 1930s were the start of the golden age of film musicals, the arrival of which brought to an end the age of operetta.

Zarzuela

At much the same time as operetta was developing in Paris, London and Vienna, a reaction to the domination of French and Italian opera in Spain began with the revival of the old tradition of **zarzuela** – theatrical shows that alternate between scenes spoken in prose and in verse, and musical scenes that include popular songs, operatic arias and dancing.

Some of these variety shows are risqué one-act farces, while others are more operatic in ambition. The *zarzuela* peaked in popularity in the final decades of the 19th century, but survived until the 1950s, and interest has again been shown in the genre in recent decades. Apart from Albéniz and Granados, composers of *zarzuela* are generally not known outside Spanish-speaking countries. The world-famous tenor and conductor, Plácido Domingo, began his career singing in the *zarzuela* company that his parents ran in Mexico.

7. OPERA IN THE MODERN ERA

The 20th and 21st centuries in music, as in all of the arts, have proved to be a period of great diversity and experimentation, although there have been some common trends. New operas appear far less often than in the 18th and 19th centuries, largely due to the huge cost of maintaining the high standards that the public have come to expect in modern times. Consequently, opera companies have come to rely on staging revivals of the standard repertoire to generate a regular income, supplemented by occasional co-productions of new operas that have proved successful elsewhere, and only rarely taking the risk of commissioning their own new works.

To address the problem of cost, some composers have used relatively small instrumental ensembles rather than the huge orchestras of the Romantic era. For example, Britten's comic opera **Albert Herring** (1947) requires an ensemble of only 13 players. For similar reasons, 'music theatre' pieces that can be semi-staged in small venues, such as Stravinsky's **The Soldier's Tale** (1918), have been intermittently popular.

There has also been a willingness by some opera composers to tackle a broader range of subjects, from those based on the human psyche to such contemporary topics as President Nixon's historic visit to China in **Nixon in China** (1985) by John Adams, life in a modern airport terminal in Jonathan Dove's comic opera **Flight** (1998), and the dangers of the Internet in **Two Boys** (2011) by Nico Muhly.

Richard Strauss

In 1889 the German composer Richard Strauss (1864–1949, unrelated to Johann Strauss II) was appointed music assistant at Bayreuth, where first he worked as répétiteur for a production of Wagner's *Parsifal*, and then conducted Wagner's *Tannhäuser* in 1894. Strauss was known mainly for his late-Romantic orchestral music until the production in 1905 of his first successful opera, **Salome.**

The symphonic style of the work, its huge orchestra and its use of *leitmotifs*, places *Salome* clearly in the Wagnerian tradition, although Strauss's vocal lines are much more angular than Wagner's, and his harmony is considerably more dissonant. The work is in a single act and is based on a German translation of the play *Salomé* by Oscar Wilde. It is famed for its climax in which Salome's reward for performing the dance of the seven veils is the head of John the Baptist, after whom she lusts. She kisses the severed head on the lips, causing her disgusted step-father, King Herod, to order his soldiers to kill her.

A key part of the original staging was a huge moon designed as a visual reminder that Strauss's music was intended to reflect the inner turmoil and neuroses of the opera's troubled characters. *Salome* is, in fact, a work of the expressionist movement, best known through the painting known as 'The Scream', first created in 1893 by the Norwegian artist Edvard Munch. The movement sought to express inner fears, using distortion and exaggeration to maximise the emotional impact of the work.

Strauss's next one-act opera, **Elektra** (1909), is even more stark. The text by the Austrian dramatist Hugo von Hofmannsthal (who went on to write the libretti for many of Strauss's later operas) is based on his own 1904 play of the same name, which in turn is loosely based on elements from an ancient Greek myth, as told by Sophocles. However, Hofmannsthal focuses on Elektra and Klytaemnestra, her mother and murderer of her father, Agamemnon, to the exclusion of almost everything else. As such, it provides a vehicle for

The best-known operas of Richard Strauss

Salome, 1905
Elektra, 1909
Der Rosenkavalier, 1911
Ariadne auf Naxos, 1916
Die Frau ohne Schatten, 1919
Arabella, 1933
Capriccio, 1942

another work of savage expressionism, notorious for the difficulty of its main solo parts that require extremely powerful singers to be heard above a huge orchestra that frequently plays at full volume.

Strauss abandoned extreme dissonance after *Elektra*. Indeed, his next opera, the enormously successful **Der Rosenkavalier** (The Knight of the Rose, 1911), is based on elegant melodic lines and lush, chromatic harmonies. Composers such as Strauss and Puccini who continued to develop the style of 19th-century music into the 20th century, are sometimes described as **Post-Romantic**.

Der Rosenkavalier is a three-act comedy, set in 18th-century Vienna, that includes such familiar features as waltzes and a Mozartian trouser role for Count Octavian, the toy-boy of the Marschallin, Princess Marie Thérèse von Werdenberg. Together with Sophie, Octavian's beloved, the three women sing a justly famous and ecstatically beautiful trio in Act Three, in which the Marschallin finally resigns herself to the fact that Octavian will be happier with the very much younger Sophie.

Richard Strauss's
Der Rosenkavalier,
trio

John Schlesinger's production of *Der Rosenkavalier* for the Royal Opera House, Covent Garden

Ariadne auf Naxos (Ariadne on the Isle of Naxos) started life in 1912 as a one-act opera intended to be performed at the end of a play by Molière, for which Strauss had also written incidental music. The combination proved over long, and in 1916 Hofmannsthal and Strauss produced a new version of *Ariadne*, in which a prologue sets the scene. A company trying to rehearse the serious opera *Ariadne auf Naxos* constantly gets in the way of a troupe rehearsing a comedy. Chaos ensues when it is announced that tragedy and comedy must be combined into a single performance to leave time for a firework display. The result is the one-act opera originally heard in 1912. The work contains several humorous caricatures of opera singers, and Strauss includes a veritable historical anthology of operatic styles in his music.

Die Frau ohne Schatten (The Woman without a Shadow) has, ever since its first performance in 1919, divided critical opinion. It is long, complex, difficult to stage and requires a huge orchestra, but contains some of Strauss's finest music.

For their final collaboration, **Arabella** (1933), Hofmannsthal and Strauss reverted to the lyric-comedy formula (and Viennese setting) that had made *Der Rosenkavalier* such a success. By now, Strauss was writing for a more modest orchestra (about the size of that used in the 1860s, in which period the work is set). Superficially the opera may seem sentimental but it is centred on an astonishingly dysfunctional family, who try to reverse their declining fortunes (resulting from compulsive gambling) by passing off their youngest daughter as a boy in order to leave the way clear to marry off her elder sister (Arabella) into money. Many misunderstandings and confusions take place before the resolution of a happy ending.

Strauss's last opera is in a single act and has a text derived from several authors, including the composer himself, but mainly completed by the conductor Clemens Krauss. Fittingly for a final opera written at the age of 78, **Capriccio** (subtitled 'A Conversation Piece for Music') centres on the relationship between poetry and music, set in the context of late-18th-century Paris. The work was first performed in Munich in 1942, conducted by Krauss, just a year before the opera house was destroyed by bombing in the Second World War.

Debussy and Bartók

While Strauss's debt to Wagner is hard to miss in his operas, the French composer Claude Debussy (1862–1918) went to considerable lengths to deny any Wagnerian influence on his only completed opera, **Pelléas et Mélisande** (1902). This was in part political, for Debussy argued that the increasing influence of Wagner on some of his fellow composers was a threat to the character of French music.

Despite such protestations, Pelléas was through-composed like a Wagnerian music drama, elements of its plot are similar to the story of Tristan und Isolde, and Debussy made extensive use of leitmotifs in the work, although of a far less sharply-defined nature than those of Wagner. However, Debussy's sound-world is very different from that of Wagner. The French composer frequently makes use of unusual scales and timbres, and his chromatic chords are generally used as static points of colour rather than as part of far-reaching harmonic progressions.

In fact, the word 'static' describes many aspects of Pelléas. It is set in an unspecified ancient time in a place called Allemonde (all the world). It opens with Prince Gollaud, lost in a forest, stumbling upon Mélisande, who is also lost and crying because she has lost her crown in a well. When Gollaud attempts to retrieve it, she says that she would rather die than have it back. The opera is peopled by characters who are lost or blind, and who seem not to know what is happening to them or why, merely that they are somehow victims of fate.

Similarly, the opera continues to unfold with events that seem to have some as yet unknown importance. For example, Mélisande marries Gollaud but then loses her wedding ring down a well when talking to his brother, Pelléas. At that moment a clock strikes noon and Gollaud is thrown from his horse. He orders Pelléas and Mélisande to search for the ring, which she falsely claims was lost in a seaside cave. When they go there at night, a shaft of moonlight reveals three sleeping beggars.

All of this apparent obscurity arises from the opera's symbolist text by Maurice Maeterlinck. It began life as a play which Debussy himself abbreviated to form the prose libretto. Symbolist writers aimed to suggest ideas, rather than describe them directly. For example, conflicting emotions between characters might be symbolised by a storm, or the flowing cycle of life by running water.

At the first performance of Maeterlinck's play in 1893, the director used minimal lighting and placed the actors behind a huge gauze to give the work a dreamy, unworldly effect. In a similar way, Debussy's music is often described as **impressionist**, because (like impressionist painting) it focuses more on suggestion and atmosphere than on traditional formal structures or descriptive techniques.

Debussy's opera received its first performance in 1902 to mixed reviews. It did not appeal to the regular patrons of the Opéra-Comique, but enthusiasm grew among the younger opera lovers of the day and premieres in other cities (especially at Covent Garden in 1909) proved to be very successful. Nevertheless, when Richard Strauss first heard *Pelléas et Mélisande* in 1907 he famously turned to his host, the French author Romain Rolland, at the end of the first act to ask 'Is it like this all the way through?' Strauss's complaint that there was no musical development – that the work was too static – is perhaps evidence that Debussy had succeeded in shaking off the ghost of Wagner.

Symbolism also lies at the heart of the only opera by the Hungarian composer, Béla Bartók (1881–1945). *Bluebeard's Castle* was composed in 1911, but had to wait until 1918 for its first performance, a delay that allowed the composer to make several changes. Bartók's score was influenced by both Richard Strauss and Debussy, but the composer's detailed knowledge of Hungarian folk music is also apparent in the work, especially in his use of particular scales associated with that folk music.

Bluebeard's Castle is a one-act opera that lasts for little more than an hour and, while it requires a large orchestra, has only two singing parts: Bluebeard and his new wife, Judith. She arrives at his gloomy castle and asks that seven doors be unlocked to bring in the light. To her horror, each door opens to reveal a stream of symbolically coloured light, starting with blood red for her husband's torture chamber. The other doors reveal his armoury, treasury, garden, kingdom, lake of tears and finally his three former wives. The opera ends when Bluebeard crowns his latest wife and leads her through the seventh door. The seven doors are thought to symbolise the confessions of the male psyche, from cruelty and ambition to regret and the need for understanding. The work starts with a spoken prologue which advises the audience to pay careful attention as the moral of the story can apply to the real world.

Schoenberg and Berg

The earliest works of the Austrian composer Arnold Schoenberg (1874–1951) were written in the highly chromatic style of Wagner and Richard Strauss. Schoenberg soon came to believe that the expressive power of this type of writing came from its use of dissonance, and that anchoring music to a key diluted its emotional impact. Accordingly his first opera, *Erwartung* (Expectation) is **atonal** – that is, without any sense of being in a key or having a 'home note'.

Written in little more than two weeks in the summer of 1909, *Erwartung* had to wait until 1924 for its first performance. The work requires a very large orchestra, but only a single voice (a type of work known as a **monodrama**) and is often performed as a concert work. Reflecting the opera's subtitle of *Angsttraum* (Nightmare), it is an expressionist work about a frightened woman searching for her lover in a forest at dead of night. When she finds his dead body she angrily rebukes him for being unfaithful, leaving the audience to speculate about whether she was his murderer, before wandering off alone. It is never clear whether the audience has witnessed a real event, a nightmare or a psychotic symptom of an unstable woman.

The opera is in four short scenes, distinguished by different lighting, a little like the seven doorways in *Bluebeard's Castle*. Indeed, as *Erwartung* is less than 30 minutes in length, it is often paired with Bartók's opera to form an operatic double bill.

Schoenberg's last opera, **Moses und Aron**, begun in 1930, was intended to be a much more substantial work. However, the composer was never able to secure funding for its final act, and it remained unfinished at his death. Nevertheless, the first two acts were first performed in 1957 and have been staged a number of times since, despite the very large performing forces required.

Ever since the invention of opera, one of the main ways to give structure to music had been the use of related keys to create the sense of a journey away from home and back again. This was impossible in atonal music, which has no sense of key, but by the 1930s Schoenberg was using a system known as **serialism**, in which each of the 12 pitch names in western music is used in a chosen order to form a series of 12 notes that can be manipulated in a limited number of ways to create the entire piece. Because each pitch name is used only once in the 12-note series, no pitch is given undue prominence as the key note is in music that has a key. The whole of

Berg's *Wozzeck* at English National Opera

Moses und Aron is thus based on the manipulation of a single series of 12 pitches.

Schoenberg's pupil, Alban Berg (1885–1935), adopted a different approach to structuring the partially atonal music in his first opera, **Wozzeck** (completed in 1922 and first performed in 1925), which he based on a succession of short forms, listed in the table below, which are associated with instrumental music of previous centuries, albeit it in a far less dissonant style than that employed by Berg.

The libretto, adapted by the composer, is based on a set of scenes from a play called *Woyzeck* by the German author Georg Büchner, which was left incomplete at his death in 1837 at the age of only 23. It was the first literary work in German whose main characters are working class. Berg selected 15 scenes, forming them into three acts of five scenes each, with an instrumental **interlude** before the final scene. The latter is not atonal – it is composed in the key of D minor.

In addition to the various musical structures, Berg unified the work with *leitmotifs* which are associated with the main characters, and developed ideas in the symphonic style of Wagner. For example, elements of the military march heard in Act One, Scene Three, return in the last scene of that act to remind the audience that Marie has a weakness for soldiers. Similarly, the lullaby she sings in Act One is transformed to become the music she sings to her child when he becomes restless at the start of Act Two.

Act One: Five Character Pieces	
Suite	Wozzeck, a penniless soldier, is taunted by his captain for being an unmarried father. He protests that the poor cannot afford morals.
Rhapsody	Wozzeck experiences mad visions at sunset.
Military March and Lullaby	Wozzeck's partner Marie is attracted to a passing drum major. Alarmed by Wozzeck's state of mind, she sings their child to sleep.
Passacaglia	To earn money Wozzeck is experimented upon by a sadistic doctor, who is pleased to discover that his patient seems to be going mad.
Rondo	After a token struggle, Marie takes the drum major to bed.
Act Two: Symphony in Five Movements	
Sonata	Wozzeck hands Marie his meagre army pay and his pittance from the doctor, but wonders where she got her new earrings.
Fantasia and Fugue	The captain and doctor morbidly discuss sickness and death, and goad Wozzeck with rumours of Marie's infidelity.
Largo	Wozzeck confronts Marie who does not deny what has happened and tells him to knife her rather than hit her.
Scherzo	Wozzeck discovers Marie at an inn, dancing with the drum major. A drunken idiot says he smells blood and Wozzeck panics.
Rondo marziale	In the army barracks Wozzeck is woken by demented visions of a knife blade. He is beaten mercilessly by the drunken drum major.
Act Three: Six Inventions	
Invention on a theme	Marie reads the biblical account of the woman taken in adultery and tells her son a story about a deserted orphan boy.
Invention on a single note (B)	As a blood-red moon rises above a pool, Wozzeck tells Marie that if he can't have her, nobody can and then slits her throat.
Invention on a rhythm	Wozzeck dances madly with Marie's neighbour in a tavern, but rushes out when the blood on his hands is noticed.
Invention on a six-note chord	He returns to the pool to retrieve his knife, wades in too far and drowns. The captain and doctor hear this but do nothing to help.
Invention on a key	An orchestral interlude, rather than a scene, which is often interpreted as a plea for the poor of the world.
Invention on a continuous quaver rhythm	Children playing in the street outside Marie's house tell her son that his mother is dead, before running off to see the corpse. The little boy is too young to understand what has happened.

The synopsis should leave no doubt that *Wozzeck* is expressionist opera – some even describe it as a late example of *verismo*. However, it is difficult to escape the feeling that Wozzeck is as much a victim as Marie. Rather like the characters in Debussy's *Pelléas et Mélisande*, he seems to be driven by forces that he does not understand and, as such, epitomises the human dilemma of the 20th century. After its premiere in 1925 in Berlin, *Wozzeck* soon became one of the most popular works of modern music.

The orchestration of Berg's second opera, **Lulu**, was unfinished at the composer's death in 1935 and the opera had to be performed without its final act until after the death of his widow, who had forbidden completion of the scoring. The first complete performance took place in Paris in 1979.

As in *Wozzeck*, Berg generates much sympathy for the work's title character, who is driven by sexual impulses she seems unable to control. She seems to destroy almost everyone with whom she comes into contact – her first husband has a stroke, her second commits suicide, and she shoots the third, after which she finds herself attracted to a lesbian who helps Lulu escape from jail. She eventually ends up working as a prostitute in London, where her three clients are played by the same singers who portrayed her husbands in Act One. The third is Jack the Ripper, who murders both Lulu and her lesbian lover. This results in Act Three appearing as a mirror of Act One, emphasised by a central interlude in Act Two which accompanies a film in which Lulu leaves prison to an exact palindrome of the music to which she entered prison. Berg used 12-note serial technique in parts of *Lulu*, although in an unusual way in which different, but related, rows are used for different characters, almost like *leitmotifs*.

Opera in Russia: Prokofiev, Shostakovich and Stravinsky

The strong operatic tradition that developed in Russia in the 19th century, outlined in the previous chapter, continued well into the 20th century.

Sergei Prokofiev (1891–1953) travelled to the USA in 1918, partly to get away from the disruption of the 1917 Russian Revolution. While there he was commissioned by Chicago Lyric Opera to write **The Love for Three Oranges** (1919), a comedy with a very silly plot that can be traced through an 18th-century version by Carlo Gozzi (on whose work Puccini's *Turandot* was based) back to a pair of fairy stories published in 1634. As an opera in Russian would not have been understood in Chicago, and Prokofiev spoke little English, the work was originally performed in French. It had a mixed reception, and only really became popular after the Second World War.

Among Prokofiev's other operas, **War and Peace** (based on Tolstoy's monumental novel of the same name) reflected the increasing difficulty of working in Soviet Russia as officials banned the first performance of the second part of the work in 1946, despite Prokofiev's attempts to make it more patriotic, as required. The complete opera, in the form the composer intended, was not staged until 1959, six years after Prokofiev's death. Its huge cast and great length ensure that modern productions remain rare.

Few composers in Communist Russia knew more about political interference than Dmitri Shostakovich (1906–1975), who at one stage kept a packed suitcase in his flat so that if arrested he could leave without disturbing his family.

The plot of his first opera **The Nose** captures the frivolity of the 1920s and has been likened to an operatic version of a Charlie Chaplin film. The libretto, based on a satirical story about bureaucracy by the Russian writer Nikolai Gogol, concerns a civil servant whose nose leaves his face and develops a life of its own, at one point becoming a state councillor. Despite the fact that Gogol's story was written nearly a century earlier and set in pre-revolutionary Russia, the opera was attacked by officialdom and, after its initial run in 1930, was not performed again until 1974.

Much worse was to follow with Shostakovich's next opera, **Lady Macbeth of Mtsensk** (1934). It tells the story of a 19th-century woman in an unhappy marriage who falls in love with one of her husband's labourers but who is driven to murder and who eventually commits suicide. With its elements of *verismo* and expressionism, the work was initially successful until Stalin attended a performance. Shostakovich was in the audience and reportedly turned as white as a sheet after seeing the party leader's reaction to his work. Shortly after, the opera was banned and Shostakovich publicly criticised. Commissions dried up and many of the composer's friends and relatives were imprisoned or killed in Stalin's 'great terror' of 1936.

Igor Stravinsky (1882–1971) avoided the problem of state interference in his work through the simple expedient of not living in Communist Russia. After six years in Switzerland from the start of the First World War to 1920, he lived in France until the outbreak of the Second World War, and thereafter in America, where he became a naturalised citizen of the United States.

Stravinsky's best-known, and only full-length, opera is **The Rake's Progress**, first performed in Venice in 1951. The libretto by W. H. Auden and Chester Kallman is loosely based on the eight satirical engravings known as *A Rake's Progress*, created in London in the 1730s by the artist William Hogarth.

The work tells the story of the downfall of the naive and reckless Tom Rakewell, who deserts Anne Trulove for a life of luxury, gambling and whoring in London, in the company of Nick Shadow, who turns out to be the devil in disguise. After various misadventures Shadow fails to claim Tom's soul, but condemns him to madness, and Tom ends his days in Bedlam, the London hospital for the insane. In an epilogue after Act Three, each character finds their own moral in the tale, before agreeing that the devil finds work for idle hands.

The work is written in the **neoclassical** style that Stravinsky had employed since the 1920s. In the case of *The Rake's Progress*, this included using a small orchestra of 18th-century proportions, separating arias with recitative (accompanied by a harpsichord), and writing the part of Anne for a *coloratura* soprano. However, despite its many references to Mozartian opera, and its use of classical structures, the music is thoroughly modern, and not pastiche in style.

Janáček

The strong operatic tradition of 19th-century Bohemia extended into the new century with the works of Leoš Janáček (1854–1928). His first major success came at the age of 50, with *Jenůfa*. It was first performed in 1904 (the year in which Dvořák died) in Brno, now the second largest city in the Czech Republic.

Janáček wrote his own text, based on a bleak Czech play, and he followed the example of Gustave Charpentier's opera *Louise* (1900) by casting it in the form of a prose libretto. The story of violence and infanticide in a remote village places the work in the *verismo* tradition, and was enough to stop the work being performed at the Prague National Theatre until 1916. In fact, Janáček's operas were little known beyond the composer's own country until the Australian conductor Charles Mackerras began introducing them at Sadler's Wells Opera, now English National Opera, after World War II.

Starting in his late 60s, Janáček wrote five operas that continue to attract modern productions. **The Adventures of Mr Brouček** (1920) is a two-part comedy in which Brouček (a sort of Czech Falstaff) is first sent to the moon and is then despatched back to the 15th century – all fuelled by lashings of alcohol.

Katya Kabanova (1921) is a tragedy based on the play *The Storm* by the Russian dramatist Alexander Ostrovsky. Katya, trapped in a loveless marriage and bullied by a critical mother-in-law, falls in love with another man but is eventually driven to suicide.

The Cunning Little Vixen at Glyndebourne Opera House

The Cunning Little Vixen (1924) has a libretto by Janáček himself, inspired by a series of newspaper cartoons about a group of anthropomorphic animals, their relationship with the humans in their rural community, and nature's continuing cycle of birth, death and renewal.

Janáček's *The Cunning Little Vixen*

The Makropoulos Affair (1926) also has a libretto by Janáček, this time based on a surreal play by the Czech writer Karel Čapcek, about a 16th-century alchemist who invents a formula to extend human life by 300 years and tests it on his daughter. It is now the 20th century, she is an international opera singer and she is aging rapidly as the formula wears off. She realises that life has little value if it never ends and decides not to take any more of the formula. Nobody else wants it and, as the secret is burned, she dies saying the opening words of the Lord's Prayer.

The libretto of *From the House of the Dead* is again by the composer, and is based on a novel by the Russian author, Fyodor Dostoevsky, that portrays the life of convicts in a Siberian prison camp. It was first performed in 1930.

After Janáček's death, the vibrant tradition of Czech opera would continue in the hands of Bohuslav Martinů (1890–1959, see page 173).

From *Zeitoper* to the operatic musical

Because 19th-century operetta often parodied opera and shared some of its features, it was not greatly different musically from many of the less serious operas of the day. However, as musicals replaced operetta in the 20th century, the familiar waltz songs and patter songs of previous generations gave way to jazz- and blues-based styles of popular music emanating from America.

As musicals developed a style of their own, some composers looked for ways to create a more accessible style of opera than that exemplified by many of the works outlined so far in this chapter. One of the first was **Zeitoper** (opera of the times) which developed in 1920s' Germany. Its most famous example is ***Jonny spielt auf*** (Johnny Strikes Out, 1927) by Ernst Krenek (1900–1991), an Austrian composer of Czech origin who moved to the USA in 1938. *Jonny spielt auf* combines jazz rhythms with slightly astringent harmonies and soon became a theatrical hit of the age. Its rather implausible libretto (by the composer) is sometimes seen as an allegory of the American jazz age triumphing over German intellectualism.

Krenek's inspiration for his *Zeitoper* came from hearing Sam Wooding's jazz band from New York playing in Berlin in 1925. Also in that Berlin audience was the German composer Kurt Weill (1900–1950) who was shortly to team up with the German dramatist, Berthold Brecht, as librettist. Brecht had developed an updated form of *Singspiel* which he cheekily called '*Songspiel*' and their most famous collaboration, **Die Dreigroschenoper** (The Threepenny Opera) was first staged in 1928.

The hugely successful work is an adaptation of *The Beggar's Opera* (see page 49), largely following the same plot but updating it to the Victorian era. However, the music by Weill is almost all new, and is intended to interrupt the action and force

Weill's *The Threepenny Opera*

the listener to question their reaction to the events on stage. Like Krenek, Weill adopted a combination of jazz idioms and occasionally discordant harmony, and he scored the work for just seven players. These, rather like the musicians in the cabaret bands of the day, had to play 23 instruments between them. The structure of the work is similar to that of a *Singspiel*, with dialogue between the musical numbers, many of which are simple strophic songs with plenty of repetition in the vocal line, designed to be suitable for actors to sing rather than trained opera singers.

Die Dreigroschenoper broaches a similar subject to Berg's *Wozzeck*, first performed three years earlier – society criminalises the extreme poor, and criminality will only be eradicated by tackling poverty – although Weill conveys this message in a musical style very different from Berg's.

Brecht and Weill collaborated on several other works, including the three-act opera ***Aufstieg und Fall der Stadt Mahagonny*** (Rise and Fall of the City of Mahagonny), a political satire first performed in 1930. However, their work was banned in Germany after Hitler came to power in 1933, and Brecht and Weill had to flee the country. Weill eventually settled in the USA, where he continued to promote the idea of popular opera, notably in his 'American opera' ***Street Scene*** (1947), a work that opened on Broadway but that in recent decades has been produced by New York City Opera and English National Opera.

Germany's leading composer in the 1920s and 1930s was Paul Hindemith (1895–1963). He had already caused scandals with his triptych of one-act expressionist operas, ***Mörder, Hoffnung der Frauen*** (Murderer, Hope of Women, 1921) that seems to glorify rape, ***Das Nusch-Nuschi*** (1921), a burlesque that ridiculed *Tristan und Isolde*, and ***Sancta Susanna*** (Saint Susanna, 1922) about a sexual frenzy in a nunnery.

Hindemith's comic opera ***Neues vom Tage*** (News of the Day, 1929) is another example of *Zeitoper* – a satire of modern life and the conflict between newspapers hungry for news and celebrities wishing to have a private married life. The work includes a 'divorce duet' and parodies of the music of Puccini and of Berlin cabaret music.

In a scenario that seems to anticipate Shostakovich's brush with Stalin only a few years later, Hitler had walked out of a performance of *Neues vom Tage* in disgust at seeing a naked soprano singing from her bathtub about the joys of modern plumbing. Hindemith's work was increasingly attacked as degenerate by the Nazi propaganda machine and in 1938 he left Germany, emigrating to the USA two years later.

It was in America that a new type of 'cross-over' work was developing, spanning the gap between popular and art music. Jerome Kern's *Show Boat* had shown as early as 1927 that the musical could sustain serious drama and themes such as racial prejudice, and George Gershwin (1898–1937) had had considerable success with orchestral works such as *Rhapsody in Blue* (1924) that are now often described as 'symphonic jazz', as well as with musicals such as *Lady Be Good* (1924) and *Girl Crazy* (1930).

Gershwin's most ambitious project was ***Porgy and Bess*** (1935), a work that he described as a 'folk opera' and hoped would receive its premiere at New York's Metropolitan Opera House. In fact, it was launched on Broadway (avoiding use of the word 'opera') where it was easier to assemble the Afro-American cast that Gershwin wanted, but today it is more likely to be presented in an opera house than a theatre.

The work is based on the 1925 novel (and later adaptation as a stage play) *Porgy* by DuBose Heyward. It tells a moving story of social realism about Porgy, a crippled African-American living in the slums of Charleston in the south of the United States, and his attempts to rescue Bess from her pimp and the drug dealer Sportin' Life.

Unlike musicals of the day, *Porgy and Bess* is through-composed, making extensive use of *leitmotifs* and employing recitative for the dialogue between the main musical numbers. As in his symphonic jazz, Gershwin created an attractive amalgam of elements from contemporary classical music, popular song, jazz, blues and spirituals. However, the work's lukewarm reception was blamed partly on the fact that audiences were unfamiliar with the conventions of recitative. Also, a number of native speakers felt that Gershwin had failed to capture the inflexions of Afro-American dialect:

Gershwin's *Porgy and Bess*, 'It ain't necessarily so'

A 1942 Broadway revival replaced the recitatives with spoken dialogue and made many cuts, but most new productions today (particularly by opera companies) have tended to respect the unity and integrity of Gershwin's original concept.

Less than eight years after Gershwin's early death, a young American composer named Leonard Bernstein (1918–1990) achieved a Broadway hit with his first musical, **On the Town** (1944), a work about the antics of three American sailors on 24-hour shore leave in New York City during wartime 1944 that includes the hit song 'New York, New York'.

Bernstein's most famous musical is, of course, **West Side Story** (1957). The plot is based on Shakespeare's *Romeo and Juliet*, but without using the Elizabethan text, and it is set in 1950s' New York, with the rival families of the original becoming rival teenage gangs. It was a revolutionary work. Instead of the nostalgic romanticism of many earlier musicals, it is a story that ends in bleak despair. Extended dance sequences convey much of the drama, and in place of rousing finales, both acts end in murder.

Bernstein had wanted to write the work in a more operatic style than would have been practical for actors who sing in musicals, and it is perhaps not surprising that when he came to make an audio recording of the musical in 1984, he chose opera singers for the main roles. It is certainly a work that suits the operatic stage, and has been performed by many regional opera companies in recent years.

The five politicians from Bernstein's *Candide* in a 50th anniversary production staged in Paris at the Théâtre du Châtelet in 2006, in Milan at La Scala in 2007 and in London at English National Opera in 2008

Bernstein also wrote a short one-act opera, **Trouble in Tahiti** (1952), followed by a much more substantial work, **Candide**, first staged in 1956. Based on a satire dating from 1759 by the French writer Voltaire, Bernstein's original version was essentially a Broadway musical – and, with its rapid succession of short scenes and dense narrative, a box office disaster. Numerous revisions followed, including supplying the work with new text. By the time of a 1982 revision for New York City Opera, the work was described as an operetta. However, Bernstein then revised this for Scottish Opera in 1988. A version with a text closer to Voltaire's original was made for a production in 1999 by the UK's Royal National Theatre. Yet further changes were made for the 50th anniversary production, which saw the stage turned into a giant TV set from the 1950s, featuring modern politicians and Voltaire changing channels.

Bernstein's
Candide

The lyrics for *West Side Story*, and some additional lyrics for *Candide*, were written by Stephen Sondheim (born 1930), who has become well known as the composer of his own thought-provoking musicals. Of particular interest for this book is **Sweeney Todd: The Demon Barber of Fleet Street** (1979), a dark comedy about Todd's revenge on those responsible for his years of false imprisonment. Sondheim himself described the work as 'black operetta' and, with relatively little spoken dialogue, it has been presented in a number of opera houses.

British opera

With no native composers of international stature during most of the 18th and 19th centuries, opera in Britain largely meant foreign imports, such as the Italian *opera seria* by Handel that briefly flourished until the 1730s. The English composer Thomas Arne (1710–1778) wrote a large number of works for the stage, including **Thomas and Sally** (1760), the first comic opera in English to be sung throughout, and the **ballad opera** *Love in a Village* (1762). His setting of **Artaxerxes** (1762), to a translation of a libretto by Metastasio, was the first *opera seria* in English and continued to be performed until the 1830s. Although Arne's stage works are now occasionally revived for historical interest, he is mainly remembered for the song 'Rule, Britannia!' from his masque **Alfred** (1740).

In the first half of the 19th century, the Irish composers Michael William Balfe (1808–1870) and William Vincent Wallace (1812–1865) achieved success with now forgotten works such as Balfe's **The Bohemian Girl** (1843) and Wallace's **Maritana** (1845). In the second half of the century Arthur Sullivan (the son of an Irishman) was the great hope for serious English opera, but his popular operettas have long outlasted his one grand opera, *Ivanhoe* (1891).

The 'English musical renaissance' that began at the end of the 19th century was led by composers such as Elgar, who wrote no opera, and Parry, whose only opera was turned down by the company for whom he composed it. However, opera began to figure in the work of the next generation of composers. Gustav Holst (1874–1934) spent part of his early career playing trombone in an opera orchestra, and wrote a number of mainly small-scale operas. **Savitri** (1908) is a 30-minute **chamber opera** with a libretto by the composer that reflects his interest in Hindu spirituality. It requires three solo singers, 12 instrumentalists and an offstage wordless female chorus. Its first performance was given by amateurs, and it remains popular with student groups and small touring companies.

Hugh the Drover, the first opera by Ralph Vaughan Williams (1872–1958), also received an amateur premiere, in 1924 (some 14 years after he had started on the composition). With recitative dividing its set numbers, it has been described as a modern example of ballad opera. Vaughan Williams's next opera, **Sir John in Love,** was much more substantial. Completed in 1924, it received its first performance at the Royal College of Music in London in 1929, but had to wait until 1946 for its first professional production. Performances have been rare, but the work was re-staged by English National Opera in 2008. The libretto, by the composer himself, is based on Shakespeare's play *The Merry Wives of Windsor* and additional texts by other Elizabethan authors. Vaughan Williams makes extensive use of English folk-music idioms in the work, and specifically quotes the tune known as *Greensleeves* (which is mentioned by Shakespeare in the play on which the opera is based).

Folk music is entirely absent from Vaughan Williams's short one-act opera, ***Rider to the Sea***, premiered at the Royal College of Music in 1937. His last opera, composed on a very large scale, was ***The Pilgrim's Progress,*** produced at Covent Garden in 1951. It was not well received, and is now more likely to be heard on record or in concert performance than on the stage.

Benjamin Britten

The rather inauspicious state of English opera was blown apart on 7 June 1945, just weeks after the Second World War ended in Europe. The occasion was the re-opening of the Sadler's Wells opera house after its wartime closure with the production of a new work, ***Peter Grimes***, the first full-scale opera by Benjamin Britten (1913–1976).

Within three years *Peter Grimes* had played at 19 opera houses around the world. Britten went on to write a succession of works for the stage that have made him the most-performed opera composer born in the 20th century. Indeed, given increasing audience hostility to some of the more extreme types of musical modernism in the middle of the century, it has been suggested that opera could have become a genre of purely historic interest without the impact of Britten's contributions to the repertoire. He is justly famed for his sensitivity to setting the English language and his ability to reinvigorate and meld an eclectic mix of the best in contemporary serious music.

The idea of Peter Grimes as the subject for an opera came to Britten in 1941 when he was in the USA with his life long partner, the tenor Peter Pears (who would play the title role). There he chanced upon an article about the poetry of George Crabbe from Britten's home county of Suffolk. Pears found a copy of Crabbe's works in a second-hand bookshop, and Britten was immediately fascinated by a series of 24 poems about life in an East Anglian fishing village. Published in 1810 under the title

A selection of Britten's dramatic works

Peter Grimes (1945)
The Rape of Lucretia (1946)
Albert Herring (1947)
Billy Budd (1951)
Gloriana (1953)
The Turn of the Screw (1954)
Noye's Fludde (1958)
A Midsummer Night's Dream (1960)
Death in Venice (1973)

'The Borough', the poems are about Crabbe's birthplace of Aldeburgh on the Suffolk coast, where Britten and Pears would eventually settle and establish a world-famous music festival that continues to this day.

Crabbe's poems were written as a series of letters in verse. Britten was captivated by the dramatic possibilities of the 22nd letter, about the fisherman Peter Grimes, which told of how a closed society ganged up on an outsider – a theme that permeates many of Britten's dramatic works and that clearly resonated with his own circumstances of being a homosexual and a conscientious objector to war.

Britten and Pears worked on a draft of the libretto (which is only loosely based on Crabbe's work) before and during the difficult wartime sea crossing back to England in 1942. Montagu Slater, who had worked with Britten on earlier projects, was appointed as the official librettist and revamped the role of Grimes as a more sympathetic character than that in Crabbe's original poem, moving the suspicion of guilt for the final outcome onto the voracious crowd.

The music, mostly composed during 1944, has an underlying structure of separate numbers that flow into a succession of continuous scenes like a late-19th-century Italian opera. Duets, ensembles and choruses have a central role. All of this added to the opera's appeal to audiences who were not familiar with the modernity of Britten's style. The work was a huge success. Gustav Holst's daughter, Imogen, declared that 'here at last was a real English opera'.

featured opera

Peter Grimes has no overture and begins with a prologue consisting of an inquest into the death of fisherman Peter Grimes's young apprentice. The townsfolk clearly think that Grimes is guilty of the boy's death, but he is released with a warning to get an adult rather than a boy to help him in future. Ellen Orford, Peter's only friend, comforts him as he rages against the gossiping tongues of the community.

The first part of the prologue is set in the *arioso*-like format of 19th-century Italian opera, with the main melodic material in the orchestra, although the musical style is much more modern. Staccato woodwind motifs capture the excitement of the crowd, official court proceedings are set to monotones, Grimes gives his evidence in measured notes accompanied by low strings, and the part for the presiding lawyer includes wide leaps to underline his pompous sense of self-importance. The short duet at the end of the prologue is marked by Britten as 'recitative'. It is unaccompanied

Britten's *Peter Grimes*, Prologue and first Sea Interlude.

and bitonal, with Ellen in E major and Grimes in F minor, perhaps reflecting their differing attitudes to Grimes's reputation in the borough. Eventually, Grimes seems to share Ellen's optimism by moving into her key.

To cover scene changes and provide points of reflection, Britten included a number of orchestral interludes, four of which are often performed as a concert work. The first flows on seamlessly from the prologue and depicts the sea at dawn.

In Act One Grimes, ignoring the advice at the inquest, procures a new apprentice from the workhouse with the help of Ellen Orford, whom he one day hopes to marry. An approaching storm underpins an argument between

Peter Pears as Grimes and Joan Cross as Ellen Orford in the original production of *Peter Grimes* at Sadler's Wells (now English National Opera)

Grimes and Balstrode, in which the retired seafarer suggests to Grimes that it would be best to leave town. Grimes finishes the duet alone as the fearful storm breaks in the second interlude. The following scene is set in The Boar Inn that night. Townsfolk are sheltering from the hurricane and Grimes is drunkenly accused of murder. To calm the atmosphere everyone sings a round, *Old Joe has gone finishing*, set to a lolloping rhythm of seven beats to the bar, but the song is wrecked when Grimes tries to join in. Ellen and the new apprentice arrive, half drowned, and Grimes takes the boy off to his hut.

Act Two begins with the third interlude, 'Sunday Morning', at the end of which a church bell calls the townsfolk to worship. While the church service is heard offstage, Ellen talks to the new apprentice. As the congregation intone 'We have erred and strayed from thy ways like lost sheep' Ellen notices a tear in the boy's coat. As they recite 'We have done those things which we ought not to have done' she sees that the boy has a bruise and realises that he has already been beaten by Grimes.

Grimes rushes on, he has seen a big shoal of herring out at sea and needs his new apprentice to help bring it in. Ellen confronts Grimes about the bruise and tells him that they can have no future together. Grimes, confused and angry, strikes her and drags the boy away as the congregation are ironically heard to sing 'Amen' at the end of the service.

The argument has been overheard, rumours circulate and after malicious cries of 'Grimes is at his exercise!', the men leave to find the fisherman.

Another interlude follows, cast in the form of a passacaglia (variations over a repeating bass). The repeating melody in the bass is in fact derived from Grimes's final phrase, 'God have mercy on me'.

Peter Grimes and the boy are in his fisherman's hut on the cliff top when they hear the vengeful crowd approaching. As they get nearer, Grimes sends the boy out of back door to his fishing boat below, but the cliff was eroded in the storm, and the boy falls to his death as the townsfolk hammer on the front door. Grimes hesitates and then climbs down the cliff so that when the men burst in, everything seems normal. They all leave the way they came except Balstrode who, noticing the back door and something on the shore, follows the route that Grimes had taken minutes earlier.

An interlude depicting moonlight on the sea leads to the start of Act Three. This takes place several nights later, when a barn dance is taking place in the hall on the seafront. An offstage band can be heard playing dance music in the background (another reminder of how Britten used familiar features of Italian Romantic opera in the work). Mrs Sedley, a local gossip, is sure that something has happened to Grimes's latest apprentice, who hasn't been seen for days. When she overhears Ellen saying that the boy's jersey has been washed up on the beach, and with the knowledge that Grimes has returned from sea, Mrs Sedley is convinced that the boy has been murdered and rouses the townsfolk to a terrifying state of hatred. The curtain falls to their cries of 'Peter Grimes!' as they prepare to hunt him down.

A sixth interlude, depicting fog floating in from the sea, leads into a 'mad scene' (yet another resonance from Italian Romantic opera). Grimes appears out of the mist, clearly deranged and singing fragmentary motifs heard earlier. The ominous boom of a foghorn (played by an offstage tuba) and the distant sounds of the crowds still calling his name can be heard in the background and echo around his head. Balstrode and Ellen enter, the music dies away and Britten briefly turns to spoken dialogue as Balstrode instructs Grimes to sail far out to sea and then sink his boat.

As dawn starts to break, the Borough comes back to life, to a reprise of the first interlude, as if nothing has happened. A report from the coastguard that a ship is sinking far off the coast is dismissed as 'one of those rumours'. Everyone goes about their work, indifferent to the suicide of Peter Grimes.

Despite its dramatic impact, this ending has always been seen as problematic. Grimes may have been harsh and negligent towards his apprentices, but he was not a murderer, and so he seems to accept death as the inevitable result of being a social outcast – something that was perhaps more plausible in earlier times than it seems today. In 1948 Britten indicated that the opera is essentially an allegory of 'a subject very close to my heart – the struggle of the individual against the masses. The more vicious the society, the more vicious the individual.'

The Rape of Lucretia (1946) received its premiere at Glyndebourne Opera in 1946, just over a year after *Peter Grimes*. It is a chamber opera that requires eight singers and 13 instrumentalists, and could thus hardly be more different from the grand-opera scale of *Peter Grimes*.

In fact, during the austere years following the Second World War, production of new large-scale operas was enormously difficult. Britten, Pears, Joan Cross (who had played Ellen in *Peter Grimes*), Eric Crozier (who had directed *Peter Grimes*) and the artist John Piper (who designed *Lucretia* and many of Britten's later operas) formed a company called the English Opera Group, to present small-scale operas by Britten and other, mostly British, composers.

Albert Herring (1947) is Britten's only comic opera. The libretto by Eric Crozier is based on a short novel by the French writer Guy de Maupassant, transferred to an imaginary small town in Suffolk and revealing a very different type of community to that of *Peter Grimes*. Once again, an ensemble of only 13 instrumentalists is required. Despite the modest scale of the English Opera Group's work, touring was expensive and in 1948 Britten and Pears created the Aldeburgh Festival as a base for the company's work, with chamber opera produced in the very cramped conditions of the town's Jubilee Hall – originally little more than a village hall.

The first part of **Let's Make an Opera** (1949) is a play, in which children and adults write and rehearse an opera (**The Little Sweep**), which forms the second part of the work and that includes simple songs for audience participation. The opera, in which the sweep boy Sam is sold into service and bullied like the apprentice in Peter Grimes, is a short work that can be performed separately if preferred. The text of both parts was written by Eric Crozier, but the style of the spoken-word play now seems rather quaint and today producers can choose an alternative script for the play, or write their own. Britten scored the accompaniment for just a string quartet, piano duet and a percussionist. It can be accompanied by just piano duet (with or without percussion).

Britten returned to the large stage and full orchestra for his next opera, **Billy Budd,** a work for an all-male cast which received its premiere in four-act format at the Royal Opera House, Covent Garden in 1951. Britten substantially revised the opera for a television broadcast in 1960, reducing it to two acts, and this is the version most commonly performed today. The libretto by E. M. Forster and Eric Crozier is based on a short novel of the same name by the American author Herman Melville. Set on board ship in the Napoleonic wars, it explores the struggle between good and evil when the popular new sailor Billy Budd is victimised by the ship's master-at-arms, John Claggart. When Claggart brings phoney charges of mutiny against Budd, the young sailor strikes out, and accidentally kills his superior officer. The ship's captain feels he has to sentence Budd to be hanged, a decision that haunts him for evermore.

Billy Budd was first performed as part of the Festival of Britain celebrations in 1951 and two years later Britten's **Gloriana** received its premiere at Covent Garden as part of the coronation celebrations for Queen Elizabeth II in 1953. It is based on the relationship between Queen Elizabeth I and the Earl of Essex, told in a series of set pieces. The work was poorly received in 1953 and has had a chequered history ever since.

The Turn of the Screw (1954) is a chamber opera by Britten with a libretto by Myfanwy Piper (wife of the artist John Piper), based on a ghost story by Henry James about a governess who comes to a large country house to look after two children. They seem to be possessed by the ghosts of two family servants involved in some kind of undefined evil but, despite some spine-chilling moments, it is never clear if the governess has fantasised about the whole thing (although Britten always maintained that the ghosts are real). Although the work is not serial, most of its material is derived from a 12-note theme heard near the start, helping to give the work its intensely claustrophobic atmosphere. Each of the opera's 16 short scenes is preceded by a variation of this theme, representing a screw turning the trap tighter.

Noye's Fludde (Noah's Flood, 1958) has a text based on an early 15th-century mystery play. It is designed for performance mainly by amateurs and children in a church or large hall, rather than a theatre. A small professional ensemble supports a much larger amateur ensemble of strings, recorders, bugles, hand-bells and even tuned mugs. The work includes three hymns for audience participation.

A Midsummer Night's Dream has a libretto adapted by Britten and Pears from Shakespeare's play, and was written for the opening of an enlarged Jubilee Hall in 1960. The renovation work included adding a small pit below the stage, allowing Britten to score the opera for a modestly sized orchestra. The three groups of characters in

Music Theatre

The increasing cost of opera in a century that witnessed two world wars led some composers to write works that can be semi-staged in venues smaller than opera houses. Such pieces are sometimes described as music theatre, although confusingly this is a term that is now often used to describe musicals.

One of the first examples was Schoenberg's *Pierrot Lunaire* (Moonstruck Pierrot, 1912), an atonal setting of 21 short poems about the decreasing grasp on reality of the clown Pierrot. It is a monodrama with a soloist (often in costume) who communicates in **sprechstimme** (a cross between speaking and singing) accompanied by an ensemble of five players.

Stravinsky's **Histoire du soldat** (The Soldier's Tale, 1918), written for small touring companies, is a morality play about a soldier who sells his violin to the devil in return for a book that predicts the future. It is scored for seven players, and the text is spoken by three actors: the soldier, the devil and a narrator. A dancer plays the non-speaking role of a princess.

Façade (1923) by William Walton (1902–1983) is thought by some to be a parody of *Pierrot Lunaire*, consisting of settings of 21 witty poems by Edith Sitwell, recited in rhythm and accompanied by six players. There is no use of *sprechstimme*, though, and some of the music draws on popular styles of the day.

Eight Songs for a Mad King (1969) by Peter Maxwell Davies (born 1934) is another monodrama that is often semi-staged. It is written for a baritone soloist who is required to use many unusual and demanding vocal techniques, and the accompaniment is for six players (the same quintet as *Pierrot Lunaire*, plus a percussionist).

In the 1960s, Britten wrote three works for modest resources that he described as 'church parables' as they were all first performed in Orford Church in Suffolk and are all based on religious themes. They are intended for professional performance, unlike the composer's *Noye's Fludde*, and are played in costume with simple staging. **Curlew River** (1964) is based on a 15th-century Japanese *Noh* play, a type of classical Japanese musical drama, transferred to a medieval fenland setting in East Anglia. As in so many of the composer's dramatic works, the protagonist (a mad woman, played by a man in the *Noh* tradition) is an outsider. **The Burning Fiery Furnace** (1966) is based on the old testament story of God saving Shadrach, Meshach and Abednego from being burnt alive. **The Prodigal Son** (1968) is based on the New Testament parable. Each of the church parables requires an ensemble of only seven or eight instrumentalists, who generally play in costume.

Music theatre works are not all on a small scale. Bernstein's **Mass** was written to be performed as part of the opening ceremony of The John F. Kennedy Center for the Performing Arts in Washington, D.C. in the United States, named in honour of the late President Kennedy. It is based on a setting of the Latin Mass (acknowledging Kennedy's Roman Catholicism) in the course of which some of the participants start to doubt their faith. At the climax, the priest conducting the service throws down the sacred bread and wine in fury, before admitting to his own tiredness and doubts. The spirit of faith quietly returns and the mass ends in peace. The work calls for soloists, three choirs, altar servers, a full classical orchestra, a rock band, a marching band and four-channel pre-recorded music on tape.

the work are delineated musically by bright harps, keyboards and percussion for the fairies, romantic strings and wind for the lovers, and low woodwind and brass for the rustic characters. The part of Oberon is written for a countertenor.

Britten's musical style markedly changed in his final dramatic works, including the far-eastern influences in the three church parables (see page 169), the hints of serialism in **Owen Wingrave**, an opera for television (1971) and **Death in Venice** (1973). The last of these has a libretto by Myfanwy Piper, based on a short novel of the same name by the German author, Thomas Mann. It tells the story of a great writer who is perplexed, then humiliated and finally destroyed by his passion for a young Polish boy. The latter is played by a non-singing dancer who performs to exotic music that conjures up the sound of the Balinese gamelan.

Old and new directions

The scale of Benjamin Britten's achievement can be measured by the fact that, of the seven operas written between 1943 and 1973 that became convincingly established in the permanent international repertoire, five are by Britten (*Peter Grimes*, *Billy Budd*, *The Turn of the Screw*, *A Midsummer Night's Dream* and *Death in Venice*).

The other two are Stravinsky's 1951 neoclassical work *The Rake's Progress* (see page 155) and the post-Romantic **Dialogues des carmélites,** by Britten's friend, the French composer Francis Poulenc (1899–1963), first performed in 1957. Based on a true story of religious persecution during the French revolution, it tells the story of Blanche, a nervous young woman who joins a convent to escape from her fears of the world. As the revolutionaries get closer and the nuns take a vow of martyrdom, Blanche is overwhelmed in terror and runs away, denying any association with the convent. The nuns are arrested and sentenced to death. In a heart-rending final scene they process to the guillotine singing the *Salve Regina* louder and louder, as each nun in turn is beheaded with a thud of the blade. Blanche watches from the crowd and then, as the moral courage she always desired overwhelms her, she comes forward to die with her sisters.

Poulenc's
Dialogues des carmélites

Other new operas in the post-war years have sometimes had a chequered history and have often not travelled well beyond the country in which they were written. The Italian-American composer Gian Carlo Menotti (1911–2007) was awarded the Pulitzer Prize for music for his first full-length opera, **The Consul** (1950). Its very contemporary story of political refugees is told in a Puccini-like post-Romantic style.

The only significant opera by the major American composer Aaron Copland (1900–1990), **The Tender Land** (1954), was intended as a work for television, but was not accepted for broadcast and subsequently failed on stage, probably because of being conceived for the much more intimate nature of television.

Walton's **Troilus and Cressida** (1954) was not well received at its premiere, although later productions (for some of which the composer made revisions to the score) fared rather better. Walton subsequently felt that the initial poor reception was due to the rather old-fashioned, lyrical nature of the work in an age of modernism.

Most of the operas of the English composer Michael Tippett (1905–1998) had a mixed reception and have not attracted great interest since the composer's centenary in 2005. Critics found **The Midsummer Marriage** rather obscure despite some fine music (1955, with libretto by the composer). The first performance of **King Priam** in Coventry (1962) was eclipsed by the premiere of Britten's colossal *War Requiem* in the same city the following day. **The Knot Garden** (1970) reflects Tippett's love of jazz and the blues, but now seems rather dated by its focus on American culture of the 1960s. **The Ice Break** (1977) suffered from production difficulties and its libretto (by the composer, as usual) was criticised as sensationalist for its focus on race riots and drug-taking.

The first full-length opera by Richard Rodney Bennett (1936–2012), was **The Mines of Sulphur** (1965). The work, commissioned by the Aldeburgh Festival and dedicated to Benjamin Britten, is based on the play *Scarlet Ribbons* by Beverley Cross. The composer's experience in writing film music provides a very atmospheric backdrop to this gothic murder story. The work was enormously popular when it first appeared, with productions across Europe as well as in London and America, but has seldom been produced since 1975.

Taverner (1972) by Peter Maxwell Davies is supposedly based on the life of the 16th-century English composer John Taverner, although the chilling story of his abandonment of music in favour of religious fanaticism is now known to be untrue. The work, which is regarded as one of Maxwell Davies's most important achievements, explores thematic material written by Taverner, but the opera's complexity has ensured that productions are very rare.

Harrison Birtwistle (born 1934) studied with Maxwell Davies at Manchester University and caused a sensation when the violent antics of glove puppets were transferred to flesh and blood in his chamber opera, **Punch and Judy** (staged by the English Opera Group at the Aldeburgh Festival in 1968). Several of his full-scale operas have proved popular, especially **The Mask of Orpheus** (1986) which deals with the nature and meaning of myth by examining the contradictions in the Orpheus legend. More recently his opera **The Minotaur** (2008) is again based on the re-telling of myth.

Where the Wild Things Are (1980) by Oliver Knussen (born 1952) has a libretto by Maurice Sendak, based on his children's book of the same title. The parts for the wild characters are sung by amplified offstage voices while dancers play their parts on

Knussen's *Where the Wild Things Are*

stage. Although intended as an opera for children, the work has been described as more like memories of childhood for adults, with its rich visual imagery and textures of evocative sounds.

Le Grand Macabre (1974-77, revised 1976) is the only opera by the Hungarian-born György Ligeti (1923–2006). It is a dark and surreal comedy about a crazy world, with a focus on death and sex, that makes reference to a collage of operatic styles. The work has proved surprisingly popular, perhaps because its astringent modernist style and fast pace particularly suits the slapstick humour and absurd scenarios.

Ligeti left Hungary in 1956, shortly after the country's revolution was suppressed by the Soviet army, and eventually arrived in Cologne where he worked for a few years with Karlheinz Stockhausen (1928–2007), one of the leading exponents of electronic music. Stockhausen's most ambitious project was **Licht** (Light), a cycle of seven operas which took 27 years to complete and would require 29 hours to perform, should it ever prove practical to stage the complete cycle. Luckily, individual operas (and even individual sections of an opera) are designed to be performed as separate works.

Each opera is named after a day of the week, linked to the astrological entity after which the day is named (the sun for Sunday, the moon for Monday and so on). The first of the cycle to be performed was **Donnerstag aus Licht** (Thursday from Light, 1981), which focuses on the life of Michael, a cosmic hero. The work includes parts for an invisible choir (which are of such complexity that they have to be pre-recorded) and it ends with a 'farewell to Thursday', performed by five trumpeters in costume standing on floodlit balconies and rooftops outside the opera house. They begin playing as the last scene of the opera ends and, at the first production in Milan, they finished at midnight, marking the end of Thursday.

Minimalism

Despite the popularity of some works, the increasing complexity of modernist music, with its vocabulary of unfamiliar sounds, seldom appealed to the public at large. From quite early in the 20th century a few composers had realised that 'less can mean

Opera for television

It was not long after television became common in the home in post-war America, that television companies began commissioning chamber operas for broadcast from the studio. Although relaying works direct from an opera house is now preferred for TV broadcasting, studio commissions resulted in several important works.

The first was **Amahl and the Night Visitors** (1951) by Menotti, commisioned by NBC. It tells a touching story of a disabled boy who meets the three kings on their way to take gifts to the baby Jesus. He has nothing to give but the crutch on which he depends to walk, but when he does so his leg is miraculously healed. The opera was frequently broadcast at Christmas (and sometimes still is), and is also sometimes performed on stage by amateur and youth groups.

The Marriage (1953) by Martinů, is a comic opera in two acts, based on a play of the same name by the Russian dramatist Gogol. It was another NBC commission and was subsequently adapted for stage production.

As mentioned earlier, **The Tender Land** (1954) by Copland was intended for television, but in fact was first produced on stage.

The Flood (1962) is a biblical drama by Stravinsky in serialist style. The libretto is by his friend Robert Craft and draws on the Book of Genesis, and on medieval mystery plays from England, to tell the story of Noah. The work, which is about 30 minutes in length, was commissioned by CBS Television.

Der Zauberspiegel (The Magic Mirror) is a fairy-tale opera by the Austrian born American composer, Ernst Krenek (1900–1991), first broadcast on German television in 1967.

Britten's penultimate opera, **Owen Wingrave** (1971) was commissioned for television by the BBC. The libretto by Myfanwy Piper is based on a short story by Henry James. The work reflects both Britten's pacifist beliefs, and the theme of the destruction of a loner that permeates a number of his dramatic works. It tells of a young man who rebels against his family's tradition of military service. He is treated with contempt by his relatives, and his girlfriend taunts Owen to prove that he is not a coward by sleeping in a room in the ancestral home that is said to be haunted by a Colonel Wingrave and his son, who was killed by his father for refusing to fight. Owen agrees and is locked in, but later when cries are heard and the door is unlocked, the young man is found dead on the floor.

more', a trend reflected in post-war 'minimal art' in which painters such as Mark Rothko were celebrated for works consisting of arrestingly simple blocks of colour.

By the 1960s, the musical equivalent was starting to appear in pieces based on cells of only a few notes that were hypnotically repeated to form slowly changing patterns as they overlapped and gradually metamorphosed. The resulting harmonies can sometimes sound only gently discordant, and the pulse was generally steady, forming a totally different soundworld to that of modernist music.

Minimalism quickly became a success with the public, not least because some of its principles started to appear in pop music (initially with Mike Oldfield's *Tubular Bells* album of 1973). In return, some minimalist composers used the techniques of pop music, such as tape loops and amplified instruments.

American composers took the lead in minimalism and, despite the composer's dislike of the term, its first significant use in opera was in **Einstein on the Beach** (1976) composed by Philip Glass (born 1937) in collaboration with the avant-garde director and designer, Robert Wilson. The work is designed as a series of tableaux rather than as a narrative, and includes spoken and chanted texts, singers positioned in the orchestra pit, and characters on stage using mime and dance. It is scored for the relatively modest resources of The Philip Glass Ensemble, based on electric keyboards and a small number of amplified instruments. *Einstein on the Beach* is in four acts, separated and framed by interludes, and lasts for five hours without intervals, although the audience is invited to enter and leave whenever they wish, making the work seem more like installation art, with music supporting a series of stage images.

Glass followed his first opera with two others that are far less abstract and that form, with *Einstein*, a trilogy about men who have changed the world. **Satyagraha** (The Force of Truth, 1980) is about the life and influence of Mahatma Gandhi, and is scored for an orchestra of strings and woodwind, with no brass or percussion. **Akhnaten** (1984), tells the story of an Egyptian Pharaoh (father of Tutankhamun) who attempted to introduce monotheistic religion to his country. The work is given a deep, rich colour through being scored for orchestra without violins (necessitated by the small orchestra pit in the theatre in which it was first performed).

Glass has written 11 more operas since *Akhnaten*, including **The Perfect American** (about Walt Disney) and **The Lost** (both 2013).

John Adams (born 1947) was well known as a minimalist composer before the production of his first opera, **Nixon in China**, in 1987. The work, which includes an eclectic blend of styles, returns to the idea of a narrative structure, rather than the type of plot based on abstract concepts that had become increasingly common at the time. The libretto by Alice Goodman is based on the historic visit to China of American President Richard Nixon in 1972. Despite mixed reviews from critics, the opera has frequently been performed around the world and is popular with the public, perhaps because its story is recent enough to be well known and relevant. It may also be due

The opening scene of *Nixon in China* by John Adams (English National Opera)

to the way in which *Nixon in China* reflects traditional opera in spectacular scenes such as the Americans' entry by plane in the first act, the modern take on a *brindisi* in the banquet of endless toasting at the end of the same act, and the inclusion of a ballet sequence (of a Chinese political nature) in Act Two. Such large-scale ensemble scenes contrast with more intimate moments that capture the private exchanges between Nixon and Chairman Mao, and that explore the motivation of each leader.

Events in recent history have also been the subject of later operas by John Adams. **The Death of Klinghoffer** (1991), again with a libretto by Alice Goodman, is based on the 1985 hijacking of a sea-going liner by the Palestine Liberation Front. The PLF held the crew and passengers hostage with the intention of securing the release from prison of 50 Palestinians. When their demands were not acceded to, they killed Leon Klinghoffer, a retired and disabled American Jew who was celebrating his 36th wedding anniversary by taking a cruise on the liner with his wife. They then had his body and his wheelchair thrown overboard. The subject is treated in a much more reflective way than *Nixon in China*, with meditative monologues and a commentary from a chorus that does not participate in the action, resulting in some critics suggesting that the work might be more suited to the concert hall than the stage.

John Adams's third full-scale opera, **Doctor Atomic** (2005), similarly focuses more on characters than events, this time in the context of the fears and anxieties of those such as the physicist J. Robert Oppenheimer who tested the first atomic bomb in 1945. Several sections of the opera are more lyrical than minimalist in

Adams's *Doctor Atomic*, 'Batter my heart'

style, with the aria that ends Act One, Oppenheimer's 'Batter my heart' (a setting of a 17th-century poem by John Donne) frequently being cited as a fine example of a modern operatic lament.

Adams's librettist, Alice Goodman, withdrew from the project after a year, and the text was eventually assembled by the American stage director Peter Sellars, who had worked with Adams on his previous operas. The libretto, based on historical documents interleaved with poetry, has been the subject of considerable criticism. Although the opera continues to be performed, it is perhaps significant that in 2007 the composer adapted significant parts of the work to form a symphony for the concert hall.

Postmodernism

In music, postmodernism is a 'catch all' label often used to describe the works of a period (from about 1975 onwards) rather than any specific music style. Minimalism has played an important role in that period, but postmodernism also embraces other styles. These range from such late examples of modernism as the only opera by the French composer Olivier Messiaen (1908–1992), **St François d'Assise** (St Francis of Assisi, 1983), an austere work that requires huge performing resources, to Ligeti's *Le Grand Macabre* with its brilliant collage of different styles.

The jagged melodic lines and dissonant harmonies of 20th-century modernism, so powerful in expressionist operas, mysteries and psychological dramas, were poorly suited to the needs of comic opera which, with a few rarely performed exceptions, virtually disappeared for much of the 20th century. The exciting soundworlds of the *avant garde* do not readily allow for two important cognitive experiences in the fast-moving world of comic opera – material memorable enough to form 'signposts' that mark out structure, and a style that is familiar enough to the average listener to create a sense of anticipation.

Both of these experiences were more easily fulfilled in postmodernist works that are sometimes described as 'crossover' in style because they draw on a wide range of traditions, from pop and jazz to world music and classical minimalism.

One of the most successful modern comic operas is *Flight* by the British composer Jonathan Dove (born 1959). It had its official world premiere in 1999 at Glyndebourne, having first been presented by Glyndebourne Touring Opera in September 1998. It was revived at Glyndebourne in 2005, has been televised by Channel Four and has also been performed in America, Australia and several European countries.

The work is in three acts, with an ingeniously rhymed libretto by the British dramatist, April De Angelis, and is based on the real story of a refugee who was legally unable to leave an airport for many years. De Angelis expands this into a story about the interactions of characters trapped together for 24 hours in a terminal building.

Act One opens at dawn with the airport controller in her tower above the terminal. She announces her preference for the orderliness of the skies to scurrying passengers in a high coloratura line that reflects her physical position as well as superior attitude. The refugee, who has no name, is a countertenor who joins with her in uneasy duet, for he depends on people for food and has no interest in her planes. The unusual voice types isolate these two from the other characters in the work.

Gradually the other characters are introduced as the terminal opens and starts to fill with people. First are Bill and Tina, hoping to revive their flagging marriage with the aid of an overseas holiday and a sex manual. At intervals the tinkly chimes of an airport terminal are heard, followed by the controller giving out her streams of instructions: 'Luggage left alone unloaded will be immediately exploded.'

Next to arrive is an older woman in dark glasses, who is there hoping to meet an incoming passenger – the toy boy she had met on an earlier holiday, who of course never does arrive. She is followed by an over-sexed air steward and stewardess who enter singing 'welcome' to everyone in sight before disappearing for a quick few minutes together in the lift. The controller quickly decides to 'put a stop to that kind of thing' and announces that all stewards must report to departure.

The final couple to enter are late for their flight. Minskman is relocating to the city of Minsk on a new diplomatic mission while his heavily pregnant wife hates the very idea. As the controller

Dove's *Flight*

announces 'The very last call of all' for their flight, and the chugging minimalist texture becomes increasingly frenetic, Minskwoman cries out 'No! I don't seem able to go'. The orchestra begins a fearsome rumbling and the sound of the plane taking off without her is heard. In something resembling a modern *imbroglio* finale, the steward and stewardess are discovered in a state of undress behind a pile of suitcases before

Flight by Jonathan Dove (Vlaamse Opera, Belgium)

everyone breaks into a patter-style ensemble about the joys of flying away on holiday. Suddenly a flash of lightning is followed by a 'ding dong' from the controller, who announces that all further flights are cancelled due to approaching storms.

In Act Two, everyone is stranded in the terminal for the night. The controller leaves her tower to lament the lack of planes and the refugee gives the various women a 'magic stone' that he claims will cure their problems. Meanwhile, Bill decides to make his sex life more adventurous by chatting up a person in a sleeping bag who he thinks is the stewardess. It turns out to be the steward who, totally unbothered, takes Bill up to the now deserted control tower for a steamy lesson as the storm rages.

The women gradually get drunk and realise that they've all been duped with a 'magic stone'. They turn on the refugee in a rage, knock him unconscious by throwing their stones at him and then hide his body in a trunk.

Act Three opens at dawn the next morning, with the storm abated and everyone still trying to make sense of what happened during the night. Preceded by her chime, the controller announces an incoming flight. The older woman's 'fiancé' has not come, but the plane has brought back Minskman, who realised that his wife is more important than his diplomatic posting. Then, when Bill drops his sleeping bag to reveal he is in his underpants and the steward enters wearing Bill's trousers, a classic comic opera ensemble develops as everyone demands to know what's going on. Tina realises and knocks her husband out with a book. 'Not another one,' exclaims the older woman as the refugee's groans are heard from within the trunk. The Minskwoman suddenly goes into labour and gives birth in the airport terminal.

The start of a tiny new life transforms everyone as they reflect on their own circumstances. The refugee comes round and, on the point of being arrested by an immigration officer, tells the heart-rending story of why he has no documentation. He and his brother hid within the wheel housings of a plane to escape persecution. The refugee is still waiting for his brother, but the immigration officer tells of how a frozen body was seen falling from the plane that day. He adds that he can only help by turning a blind eye to the refugee staying in the terminal.

When Bill comes round, he can't recall what happened the previous night, and he and Tina go off on holiday, determined to bring the fun back into their marriage without manuals and rule books. The older woman decides to enjoy herself on a new holiday – and perhaps meet a new friend in the process. Minskwoman resolves to go to Minsk with her husband and new baby, and the steward and stewardess make up. All of which seems like the neat tying-up of loose ends found in the finale of any traditional comic opera. However, after everyone else has left to catch their flights, the controller and refugee are still on stage together, as they were at the start of the opera. The refugee continually repeats the words 'This is my home now' with the controller, both musically and physically, singing high above him. As the opera quietly ends with him asking the controller what she is thinking, the audience is left realising that even their relationship has changed, with the refugee now as permanently wedded to the airport as the controller.

The success of *Flight* is partly due to the brilliance of its libretto by April De Angelis, in which farce rubs shoulders with moments of great poignancy, in a contemporary setting to which most members of the audience can easily relate. However, Dove's approach to the work is equally important. Like Britten in *Peter Grimes*, he adopts a structure in which through composition barely disguises a traditional number opera of lyrical arias, duets and ensembles that contrast with such classic operatic features as its very effective 'storm music' and such novelties as the musical realisation of the take-off of a jet-engined aeroplane. There seems little doubt that audiences find this type of approach more rewarding than the continual recitative, or at least constant *arioso*, of much modernist opera.

However, *Flight* is no pastiche of 19th-century comic opera. There is no chorus and each of the three acts offers its own distinctive emotional atmosphere. It is, though, a very accessible opera, doubtless in part due to Dove's experience in community opera. As one newspaper reviewer wrote of *Flight*, 'this was a piece that made opera look like a thriving art form and not an elegant fossil'. Only time will tell if it will be a pointer to comic opera in the future.

Nixon in China by John Adams led to a genre that has become known as 'newsreel opera', based on real events in the modern world. Thomas Adès achieved considerable success with **Powder Her Face** (1995), a chamber opera about the Duchess of Argyll, whose sex life (revealed during a lurid divorce trial) scandalised Britain in the 1960s. More recently, **Anna Nicole** by Mark-Anthony Turnage (2011) is about the Playboy model who married a dying billionaire, 62 years her senior, only to become embroiled in a lengthy court case about her inheritance before dying herself of an overdose of drugs. The opera was televised in the month after its Covent Garden premiere, and received its first performance in America in October 2013 (where it became the last work to be staged by New York City Opera, which closed that same month). **Bel Canto**, a new opera from the Peruvian composer Jimmy López, commissioned for the 2015-16 season of Chicago Lyric Opera, is in the same genre, being based on a real-life hostage crisis in Lima, Peru, in 1996.

Two boys by Nico Muhly (English National Opera)

Two Boys (2011) by the American composer Nico Muhly (born 1982) to a libretto by the dramatist Craig Lucas is a contemporary opera on a much darker subject. It tells the story of a teenage boy addicted to internet chatrooms. He gets caught up in a world populated by fictional identities who lure him with tales of sex, spies and violence into committing murder.

The work is framed as a detective mystery in which the hard-drinking and world-weary DI Anne Strawson is drawn into an unfamiliar world of internet culture and role play. She at last finds the key to solving the crime when discussing clothes and make-up with her sick mother, who observes that we all try to present ourselves as we think others wish to see us, leading DI Strawson to realise that true identity can easily be disguised on the internet in order to manipulate others.

The premiere by English National Opera made extensive use of video projection onto panels which shift during the performance, capturing the nature of the work with CCTV and webcam footage, and images of internet message boards.

Despite some criticism that the documentary style of the opera results in a work that is sometimes static rather than dramatic, a number of reviewers have commented positively on Muhly's vocal writing, which reflects his experience of singing Anglican church music as a child and his own acknowledged indebtedness to Britten, whose *Peter Grimes* he studied at an early age. The production was re-staged with changes at the Metropolitan Opera, New York, in 2013.

Sunken Garden (2013) by the Dutch composer Michel van der Aa is another work for the broadband age that includes extensive use of projection – in this case, 3D video shot at the Eden Project in Cornwall. The visual images and electronic sound track interact with live musicians in an occult mystery story about characters who share a dream of a walled garden that exists between life and death, where there is no guilt or grief, but where there is a price to be paid for cheating mortality.

Following a commission by the Aix-en-Provence Festival, **Written on Skin** (2012) by the British composer George Benjamin is based on a medieval French legend, with libretto by the playwright Martin Crimp. Written for five soloists and large orchestra, with an extensive array of percussion, it received its first London performance at Covent Garden in 2013, the success of which has resulted in a commission by the Royal Opera House for a new opera from Benjamin and Crimp for performance in 2018. Further productions of *Written on Skin* at various European and North American opera houses are in preparation and the opera has been nominated for a South Bank Sky Arts Award in 2014.

The Gospel of Mary Magdalene, with score and libretto by the Italian-American composer Mark Adamo, was commissioned by San Francisco Opera in 2008. It presents a controversial view of the relationship between Mary Magdalene and Jesus, and opened to mixed reviews in 2013.

Brokeback Mountain, a new opera by American Charles Wuorinen, opened at the Teatro Real in Madrid in January 2014. The libretto by Annie Proulx is based on her controversial short story, *Brokeback Mountain*, which also formed the basis of the award-winning epic film of the same name.

It will be many years before we know if any of these works or any other new operas will enter the permanent repertoire. Several critics thought that *Nixon in China* was an interesting novelty that had little chance of survival beyond its opening run, but it has proved to be the most popular new opera of the last 30 years, both in terms of box-office receipts and the number of productions.

Individual and corporate sponsorship of opera has become more important than ever, and opera companies are developing innovative marketing and educational initiatives to attract new audiences. These include the use of social media to promote new productions, 'behind the scenes' video clips on websites, star singers being marketed like sports personalities, and price reductions for younger opera goers. In addition, several major opera houses now make high definition relays of some of their productions available on giant screens in public spaces, in cinemas, as streamed video to watch at home, and for broadcast on pay-to-view television channels, which are bringing opera to whole new audiences across the globe.

Opera companies have responded to the challenges of the 21st century with the imaginative staging of both old and new works, often drawing on the latest stage and lighting technologies, as well as video and 3D projection, and now almost everywhere providing simultaneous translation of foreign-language works. At the same time, the enormous cost of opera is being shared by companies in different countries pooling their resources to mount joint productions, so that it is becoming an increasingly international enterprise.

There are many indications that opera continues to be a vibrant art form. The best productions are frequently sold out in advance and the number of new operas being commissioned is significantly more than it was a century ago. New opera houses continue to be built, and older ones reconstructed, with a view to providing improved facilities for audiences and performers, and making better provision for the complexities of modern productions. The growing popularity of opera in areas beyond its European roots is also a positive sign - not just in the Americas, but also in China, Japan and South Korea.

Opera will change in response to the culture and audiences of the future, but it seems likely that it will continue to be at its most successful when dealing with life's rawest emotions and greatest passions: love, jealousy, revenge, forgiveness, sex, passion, corruption, fate, power and death.

The Copenhagen Opera House, opened 2005

Photo credits

Cover: Robert Workman; *pages 14, 24, 28* Helen Bartlett, www.helenbartlett.co.uk; *pages 16, 17, 18, 21* English National Opera; *page 19* Jimmy Svensson; *page 23* Paul Terry; *pages 46, 49, 50, 58, 63, 72, 77, 78, 97, 101, 110, 113, 134, 143, 148, 157* © Robbie Jack/Corbis; *page 86* Chris Christodoulou; *page 89* Tristram Kenton; *page 121* © Eduardo Abad/epa/Corbis; *page 128* © Lea Suzuki/San Francisco Chronicle/Corbis; *page 161* Catherine Ashmore; *page 165* Angus McBean Photograph (MS Thr 581), © Harvard Theatre Collection, Harvard University; *page 175* Alastair Muir; *page 178* Annemie Augustijns; *page 180* Richard Hubert Smith; *page 183* Heinz-Josef Lücking http://creativecommons.org/licenses/by-sa/3.0/de/legalcode.

The publishers have made every effort to trace copyright holders. Please contact us regarding any omissions so that we can rectify the situation.

GLOSSARY

Act. One of the main sections of an opera or play.

Alto. Short for **contralto**, a female voice of low range.

Aria. A song for solo voice with accompaniment. See also **Aria di Sorbetto**, **Arioso**, **Da Capo aria**, **Exit aria**, **Strophic aria** and the list of baroque aria types on pages 51-52.

Aria di Sorbetto. See page 72.

Arioso. Music for solo voice that is less structured than an **aria** but more melodic than **recitative**. In opera from the 19th century onwards, arioso may also refer to a passage in which the orchestra carries the main melodic line, against which singers interject short phrases in dialogue.

Atonal. Music that lacks a tonal centre or sense of key.

Auditorium. The part of a theatre or opera house in which the audience sit.

Bacchanale. Music to depict or accompany a drunken revel (from Bacchus, the Roman god of wine).

Backstage. The area in a theatre or opera house around and behind the stage that cannot normally be seen by the audience.

Balcony. A raised level of audience seating in a theatre or opera house. Often the highest of the available raised levels.

Ballad opera. A type of 18th-century English comic drama with songs, based on popular tunes set to new words, separated by spoken dialogue.

Ballet. Dance that tells a story. Ballet scenes often featured in operas written for production in France.

Banda. A group of musicians who provide music which forms part of the action of an opera, as opposed to the musical accompaniment played by the orchestra in the pit. It may be positioned offstage in the wings (*banda interna*) or the players may be onstage in costume (*banda sul palco*).

Baritone, **bass-baritone**, **bass**, **basso buffo**, **basso profundo**. Male voices of a low pitch range. See page 27.

Basso continuo. See **continuo**.

Bel canto. Literally, beautiful singing. A smooth, light and agile vocal style associated with Italian professional singers of the 18th and early 19th centuries. The term is also applied to Italian operas of the early 19th century.

Bitonal. Music in two keys at the same time, and therefore usually discordant.

Blocking. The precise movement and positioning of characters on stage, learnt and practised by the performers in a blocking rehearsal.

Box. A small, separated part of an **auditorium**, with seats for typically between two and twelve people.

Box office. The place that sells tickets for a performance.

Breeches role (or trouser role). A part for a woman to play dressed in male clothing. In opera these characters usually represent boys or very young men, but such parts are assigned to female singers because they have much greater vocal power.

Brindisi. A drinking song.

Cabaletta. The fast final section of a two-part aria (and later of a duet or vocal ensemble) in 19th-century Italian opera. It is preceded by a slow section called the **cantabile** or **cavatina**.

Cadenza. A vocal flourish, usually improvised by the singer, at the end of an aria in the baroque period.

Cantabile. A term meaning 'song-like' but also used more specifically for the opening slow section of a two-part aria (and later of a duet or vocal ensemble) in 19th-century Italian opera. It is followed by a fast section called the **cabaletta**. See also **cavatina**.

Castrato. An adult male singer with a powerful soprano or alto range caused by emasculation before the age of puberty. Such voices were very popular in Italian opera in the period 1675–1775 but the practice died out in the 19th century.

Cavatina. Originally a short and simple song. Later used for the opening slow section of a two-part aria in 19th-century Italian opera when sung at the first entrance of a singer. Like the **cantabile** (the name for this opening section when not an entrance aria), it is followed by a fast section called the **cabaletta**.

Chamber opera. An opera that requires relatively few singers and instrumentalists, and thus particularly suitable to take on tour.

Choreographer. The person who designs the movements in a ballet.

Chorus. A group who sing together, perhaps representing soldiers, priests or party goers, as required by the dramatic situation. Usually divided into soprano, altos, tenor and bass voices. The term chorus also refers to the music sung by a chorus.

Coda. A passage of music that brings a work, or a section of a work, to an end.

Coloratura. Elaborate ornamentation in vocal music, often covering a wide or high range. See also 'coloratura soprano' on page 27.

Continuo. Short for 'basso continuo'. An accompaniment in baroque opera played by a bass instrument (such as a cello) and a chordal instrument (such as a harpsichord or lute). Later a piano (or just a solo cello) was preferred, and the role of the continuo was limited to **recitativo secco**, dying out completely in the early 19th century.

Contralto. The lowest of the female voice types (see page 27).

Coup de théâtre. Something staged for special dramatic effect or surprise.

Couplet. A song in a deliberately popular or light style in French comic opera.

Curtain call. The point just after the performance of an opera when the cast and conductor assemble on stage to acknowledge the audience's applause.

Da capo aria. An aria (solo song) in three parts in which the words *da capo* ('from the top') printed at the end of the second part instructs the performers to repeat the first section to end the piece, thus forming an ABA structure. Popular in the late baroque period, singers would embellish the melody on the repeat.

Dramatic soprano, dramatic tenor. A heavy, darkly-coloured type of voice suited to dramatic

roles and able to carry over heavy orchestral textures. See page 27.

Dress circle. A raised level of audience seating in a theatre or opera house. Usually the first level above the stalls.

Dress rehearsal. A full-scale rehearsal with use of lighting, scenery, orchestra and singers in make-up and costume. The final rehearsal before the first performance.

Duet. A piece for two voices with, in opera, orchestral accompaniment. Duets are often written for a pair of lovers or for two characters in conflict with one another.

Ensemble. A piece for several solo singers with orchestral accompaniment and sometimes including the chorus. Depending on the number of soloists, an ensemble might be a trio, quartet, quintet, sextet etc.

Entr'Acte. French for 'between the acts'. See **interlude**.

Exit aria. In 18th-century opera seria, an aria that occurs at the end of a scene, after which the singer leaves the stage to an inevitable round of applause.

Finale. The last part of an opera, or of one of the acts of an opera. It is often an extended piece in several sections, with multiple characters, in which the dramatic pace moves quickly to a climax.

Flats. Flat pieces of scenery, positioned on stage (often protruding from the wings) to give the appearance of buildings, walls etc.

Fly tower. A space extending high above the stage into which scenery and other apparatus can be raised ('flown') out of sight of the audience.

French overture. A type of instrumental introduction to an opera that was popular in the baroque period. It consisted of at least two linked sections. The first was slow and featured crisply dotted rhythms, while the second was fast and fugal (with a melodic idea that is chased through various sections of the orchestra). There might then be a repeat of the slow opening, and/or at least one section in a dance style.

Front of house. The part of a theatre or opera house used by the audience (foyer, cloakrooms, bars, auditorium etc).

Gesamtkunstwerk. German for 'union of all the arts'. A term particularly associated with the composer Wagner, who saw opera as the integration of music, poetry, drama, visual art and stagecraft.

Grand opera. A type of large-scale opera that developed in 19th-century France. Usually in four or five acts and often incorporating ballet, grand opera is typified by the use of historical subjects, spectacular crowd scenes and a large orchestra.

Heldentenor. German for 'hero tenor'. A dramatic and powerful tenor voice particularly suited to heroic roles in the operas of Wagner. See page 27.

Imbroglio. Italian for tangle. An increasingly complicated and confused situation, often dramatised in an operatic **ensemble** (particularly in a **finale**).

Impressionism. A musical style particularly associated with French composers such as Debussy in the early 20th century, in which giving the impression of light, shade, colour and atmosphere is of central importance.

Interlude. A short piece of orchestral music intended to move from one mood or atmosphere to another and/or to cover a change of scenery (and thus normally played while the stage curtain is closed). Also known as an **entr'acte** or **intermezzo**.

Intermedio. A short, semi-staged musical production presented between the acts of a theatrical performance in the second half of the 16th century and a precursor of opera.

Intermezzo. Italian for 'interval'. See **interlude**.

Italian overture. A type of instrumental introduction to an opera that was popular in the baroque period. It consisted of three sections in the order fast, slow, fast.

Leitmotif. A short musical idea, often of only a few notes, used to signify someone or something in an operatic story and to help give unity to the work. Particularly associated with the operas of Wagner.

Libretto. The complete text of an opera.

Lyric soprano, lyric tenor. See page 27.

Melodrama. In opera, spoken words and mime accompanied by orchestral music.

Minimalism. A musical style of the late 20th and early 21st centuries characterised by hypnotic repetition and the superimposition of short melodic fragments.

Monodrama. A dramatic work with only one character.

Monody. A type of musical composition consisting of a single melodic line with accompaniment that formed an important part of the earliest operas.

Mezzo soprano. A female voice of lower range than a soprano. See page 27.

Motto theme. A short musical idea that returns at certain points in an opera to remind the audience of something of dramatic significance.

Music theatre. A small-scale type of music drama that can be semi-staged in a church or concert hall rather than presented as an opera. The term is also used as a synonym for 'musical theatre', referring to stage and film musicals.

Neoclassical. A musical style of the 20th century that combines elements of the baroque and classical styles of the 18th century with features of modern music.

Number opera. An opera consisting of separate, numbered items (arias, duets, ensembles, choruses etc.) as opposed to being **through-composed**.

Opera. (Italian, from the Latin *opera*, which is the plural of *opus*, meaning 'work'). An art form in which a drama is principally or entirely sung rather than spoken.

Opéra bouffe. French comic opera of the late 19th century, featuring spoken dialogue between musical numbers. A type of **operetta**. Not to be confused with Italian **opera buffa**, which was sung throughout.

Opera buffa. Italian comic opera of the 18th and early 19th centuries, usually featuring everyday settings, and servants or other non-aristocratic characters in plots involving mistaken identities and love tangles.

Opéra comique. A type of opera that features spoken dialogue between musical numbers, popular in France in the late-18th and 19th centuries. Unlike **opéra bouffe** its subject matter is not necessarily comic (*Carmen*, the most famous *opéra comique*, is a tragedy).

Opéra lyrique. Lyric opera. A type of opera popular for a time in 19th-century France. Lighter than grand opera but sung throughout (unlike **opéra comique**).

Operetta. A fairly short type of opera in a light and amusing style, often featuring satire and including spoken dialogue between the musical numbers.

Opera seria. Literally 'serious opera'. A type of Italian opera, popular in the 18th century. Plots were usually based on mythological or ancient historical subjects and the role of the hero was usually performed by a **castrato**. Most *opera seria* have a very formalised structure based on the alternation of **recitativo secco** and (mainly **da capo**) **aria**.

Orchestra pit. A sunken area between the stage and the front row of the audience. The pit normally extends across the full width of the **auditorium** and often projects beneath the front part of the stage, providing room for the conductor and an orchestra of usually at least 65–80 players.

Overture. An orchestral piece that acts as an introduction to an opera or other theatre work. See also **French overture**, **Italian overture**, **pot-pourri overture** and **prelude**.

Parlante. A direction that a passage should be sung in a speech-like style.

Patter song. A song with a humorous text that is designed to be sung very quickly. A feature often found in **opera buffa** and **operetta**.

Post-romanticism. The continued use and development of 19th-century romanticism by some 20th-century composers.

Pot-pourri overture. An **overture** based on a selection of tunes from the opera that follows.

Prelude. An orchestral introduction to an opera that is usually shorter than an **overture**.

Premiere. The first public performance of a work. The 'opening night'.

Props. Short for 'company properties'. Movable items used on stage in a production, as distinct from scenery, costumes and electrical equipment.

Proscenium. The frame or arch that separates the stage from the **auditorium** and that provides a large 'window' through which the audience views an opera.

Quartet. In opera, a piece for four solo voices with orchestra.

Recitative. A type of vocal writing common in opera up to about 1850 with rhythms and accents that resemble speech. *Recitativo secco* ('dry recitative') was commonly used for rapid dialogue and is usually accompanied by only a keyboard instrument (or sometimes with a cello) while *recitativo accompagnato* was used to convey dramatic ideas and sometimes the speech of noble characters, and is accompanied by the orchestra.

Repertory opera. The system of a resident company preparing several operas simultaneously. Each is presented in alternation or rotation on different nights for a run of typically 6–12 performances, before being replaced by a new production. The total repertory, which includes new productions as well as **revivals** and occasionally a **premiere**, might extend to 15 or more different operas over the course of a year for a full-time company.

Répétiteur. A person who rehearses the opera chorus, coaches solo singers and provides a piano accompaniment for production rehearsals.

Reprise. A repeat, usually modified, of music heard earlier in the work. A feature often found in operetta.

Rescue opera. A type of opera popular in France and Germany in the years following the French revolution at the end of the 18th century. Typically the rescue of a political prisoner would lead to the triumph of humanistic ideals over tyrants.

Revival. The restaging of a production a year or more after its original run ceased.

Ritornello. A passage of music that returns, sometimes modified, several times during an aria or other piece. In baroque ritornello form, a complete ritornello forms an introduction to the vocal soloist. Parts of that ritornello then punctuate phrases of the aria and the complete ritornello sometimes returns at the end of the piece.

Rondo form. A musical structure in which a refrain alternates with contrasting episodes, creating a pattern such as ABACA.

Rossini crescendo. A device for creating excitement by repeating a melodic pattern in increasingly short and higher versions over a pulsating accompaniment while gradually moving from very soft to very loud (the crescendo), all the while adding more instruments. Greatly liked by Rossini who used it a number of times in many of his operas.

Scena. Italian for 'scene'. A complete dramatic unit, often for a single character, that might include **recitative**, **aria**, **arioso** and orchestral music.

Semi-opera. A spoken play with songs and dance music, popular in England in the second half of the 17th century.

Serialism. A method of composition in which all 12 notes of the chromatic scale have equal prominence and the music has no sense of key.

Sinfonia. A piece of instrumental music used as an introduction to, or interlude in, a longer work such as an opera. By the end of the 17th century a sinfonia was synonymous with an **Italian Overture**. In the 18th century the sinfonia became an independent piece of orchestral music, known in English as a symphony.

Singspiel. German for opera with spoken dialogue between its musical numbers.

Sitzprobe. German for a seated rehearsal (without scenery, lighting or costumes) when singers and orchestra rehearse together.

Soprano. The highest type of female voice. See page 27.

Sprechstimme ('speech voice') or **Sprechgesang** ('speech song') a cross between speaking and singing in which speech is pitched on given notes.

Stalls. The ground-floor seats in a theatre or opera house.

Stile rappresentativo. A simple type of vocal writing used in the early years of opera, which is more expressive than speech but less tuneful than song.

Stretta. Italian for tightening. A passage towards the end of an **aria** or **ensemble**, in which the pace is accelerated to create a climax.

Strophic aria. A song that has the same music for each verse of text.

Supernumeraries. Non-singing actors, for example to fill out numbers in crowd scenes, or specialist performers, such as acrobats or puppeteers required for particular productions. Also known as 'extras'.

Surtitles. The words of an opera (in translation if the work is in a foreign language) shown on a screen above the stage or on screens at each seat in the auditorium.

Tempo di mezzo. A section at a moderate speed often positioned between a **cantabile** (or **cavatina**) and a **cabaletta**.

Tenor. The highest of the standard male voices. See page 27.

Ternary form. A structure sometimes used for simple songs, in which the opening section is repeated (perhaps with changes) to frame a middle section, creating an ABA form.

Through-composed. An opera in which the music is continuous rather than divided into separate numbers. The opposite of **number opera**.

Trio. In opera, a piece for three solo voices with orchestra.

Trouser role. See **breeches role**.

Upper circle. A raised level of audience seating in a theatre or opera house. Often above the **dress circle** but below the **balcony**.

Verismo. Italian for 'realism'. A type of opera popular in the late romantic period, characterised by a realistic (and sometimes violent) depiction of everyday life.

Wagner tuba. A bass member of the horn family, created for Richard Wagner's operatic cycle, *Der Ring des Nibelungen*.

Wings. The spaces either side of a stage.

Zarzuela. Traditional Spanish operetta that combines spoken dialogue, popular and operatic songs, and choruses.

Zeitoper. German for 'opera of the times'. A style of opera that was briefly popular in Germany in the 1920s. Typically it featured satire, political themes, and the influence of jazz and American dance music.

INDEX OF COMPOSERS AND WORKS

Page numbers of featured operas
are shown in **bold type**